I AM

The Soul's Heartbeat

Volume 6

The Beatitudes in the Gospel of St John

Kristina Kaine

Copyright © 2013 Kristina Kaine

Published by I AM Press

Cover designed by Adriana Koulias

Cover artwork: Christ Blessing by Raphael

This book is licensed to you for your personal use. Out of respect for the author, if you would like to share it with another person please purchase an additional copy for each recipient.

I AM The Soul's Heartbeat Volume 6
The Beatitudes in the Gospel of St John

First Published as a weekly Newsletter : Aug 2006 – March 2007
Second Edition published as Kindle ebook and Paperback in April 2013.

This book is written from the insight of the author, if similar information is found in other books this is co-incidental. Quotes by other authors are referenced.

ISBN-13: 978-1490394459

ISBN-10: 1490394451

More information about the author's work and websites is listed at the end of this book.

DEDICATION

Dedicated to you, may you find you soul's heartbeat..

"Difficult, unpleasant hours come to every esoteric striver, and then it's good to have some support. We find this support in the New Testament; we find advice and support for every case and situation and in every weakness; we only have to look for it. And if we don't find it, we can comfort ourselves with the conviction that it's our own weakness that keeps us from finding the right thing but that it's nevertheless in the Bible." Rudolf Steiner From the Contents of Esoteric Classes 24 August, 1910

CONTENTS

	Introduction	i
1	Blessed are the poor in spirit	1
2	Blessed are those who mourn	12
3	Blessed are the meek	22
4	Blessed are those who hunger	35
5	Blessed are the merciful	44
6	Blessed are the pure in heart	55
7	Blessed are the peacemakers	66
8	Blessed are those who are persecuted	76
9	Blessed are you when people insult you	85
10	Author's Works	94

INTRODUCTION

Sermon on the Mount After spending a night in solemn meditation and prayer in the lonely mountain-range to the west of the Lake of Galilee *(Luk 6:12)*, on the following morning our Lord called to him his disciples, and from among them chose twelve, who were to be henceforth trained to be his apostles *(Mar 3:14, Mar 3:15)*. After this solemn consecration of the twelve, he descended from the mountain-peak to a more level spot *(Luk 6:17)*, and there he sat down and delivered the "sermon on the mount" (Matt. 5-7; Luke 6:20-49) to the assembled multitude. The mountain here spoken of was probably that known by the name of the "Horns of Hattin" (Kurun Hattin), a ridge running east and west, not far from Capernaum. It was afterwards called the "Mount of Beatitudes." Easton's Bible Dictionary

The Beatitudes or The Sermon on the Mount can be found in the Gospel of St Matthew, Chapter 5. Some sources recognise 8 Beatitudes, some 9 and others 10. These Beatitudes can be compared to Buddha's eightfold path; they can also be compared to the 10 commandments. Further to that, they can be used as a path of development for our ninefold being - this is the underlying principle used in these reflections.

It is also interesting to consider that the 10 commandments were given on a mountain. Also, at the end of the Gospel of St Matthew, in Chapter 24, Jesus speaks of the Apocalypse on the Mount of Olives.

1. Blessed are the poor in spirit, for theirs is the kingdom of heaven.
2. Blessed are those who mourn, for they will be comforted.
3. Blessed are the meek, for they will inherit the earth.
4. Blessed are those who hunger and thirst for righteousness, for they will be filled.
5. Blessed are the merciful, for they will be shown mercy.
6. Blessed are the pure in heart, for they will see God.
7. Blessed are the peacemakers, for they will be called sons of God.
8. Blessed are those who are persecuted because of righteousness, for theirs is the kingdom of heaven.
9. Blessed are you when people insult you, persecute you and falsely say all kinds of evil against you because of me. Rejoice and be glad, for your reward is great in heaven, for so men persecuted the prophets who were before you.

Emil Bock says that the Sermon on the Mount is a list of golden rules for the priesthood. The Three Years page 115.

One reader wrote:

In response to "Blessed are the Pure in Heart" I would like to quote William Blake, who when he was 8 years old saw "a tree filled with angels" on Peckham Rye in England, their bright wings "bespangling every bough like stars."

Those who are aware of Dr Steiner's work, would be aware that as the human being is in the image of God, it is the human heart which is the Sun, the other organs being the other planet of our solar system.

But the heart is the Sun. William Blake said: "What," it will be questioned, "When the Sun rises, do you not see a round disk of fire somewhat like a Guinea?" Oh no, no, I see an innumerable company of the Heavenly host crying, "Holy, Holy, Holy, is the Lord God Almighty." I question not my corporeal or vegetative eye any more than I would question a window concerning a sight. I look through it and not with it. M. F.

These Reflections were written between August 2006 and April 2007. They were written for a broad international audience as well as to be presented each Wednesday when a few people would gather to celebrate the mystery of the sacrament of bread and wine.

Soon after these Reflections concluded, Kristina's first book was published in the U.S.A "I Connecting : The Soul's Quest" by Goldenstone Press http://www.goldenstonepress.com/

Her next work explores the last book in the Bible, The Revelation, apokalupsis, as a tool for revealing how we become self-realised individuals.

Kristina says, "While the Gospel according to John has a special power to reveal our I AM to us, I think that John's Revelation, The Apocalypse, can awaken us to the power of Christ that is available within us, within the world and permeating the spiritual worlds."

March 2007

ABOUT THE TERMINOLOGY

Bible texts are taken from the Revised Standard Version of the Bible because it is one of the closest translations to the Koine Greek.

The meaning of the Greek translation of words generally comes from Expository Dictionary of New Testament Words by W. E. Vine

About the terminology used in these reflections

Esoteric Christianity recognizes the human being as a threefold being of body, soul and spirit. These three can be aligned with the three basic human faculties of will, feeling and thinking in that order.

We have our physical body in common with the mineral kingdom. Our physical body has life because of the presence of a life-force or etheric body. This force is associated with the human drive to survive; to eat, to regulate temperature and comfort, to regenerate and procreate. Humans have this in common with the plant world. An image of the function of the life forces arises when we think of an apple; on the tree it is plump, when left in the fruit bowl it gradually shrivels and rots. This depletion is the result of a waning etheric life-force. If our etheric body fully disconnects from our physical body we die. There are several Greek words in the bible that mean life and refer to our etheric body; *bios, psuche and zoe*. We could say that *bios* is physical life; *psuche* is soul life; and *zoe* is spiritual life. *Soma* is another world that refers to the etheric body. It points to etheric body that has disconnected from the physical which in its highest state is the resurrection body.

Our physical body has movement and experiences emotion because of our astral body or desire body. We have this in common with animals. For instance, plants cannot move around like animals do because they do not have this astral body. We can also call this astral part of us our soul body. If our astral body disconnects from our etheric and physical we become unconscious. In the bible the word *sarx* usually refers to our astral body. The various words for desire point to the lower or higher motives of the astral body; *thelo* – to wish, *epipotheo* - to lust, *epithumia* – to crave or covet, *eudokia* –

good pleasure.

The evolving human being refines its astral body through becoming conscious of exactly how they feel, think and will. It is the activity of these three human functions that is actually our soul. The more consciously we use these functions are the more active is our soul. *Psuche* points to the activity of the soul.

When we achieve a certain level of consciousness in our feeling, thinking and will, and only when we do, can we become aware of the human 'I'. Becoming aware of the self in its lowest and highest expressions is, in fact, our life's purpose. When we are not aware of this 'I' component in our being it works in us as a reflection, as a mirrored image. In its lower expression it is egotistical and selfish. This is a necessary part of our development because it makes us aware that we are individuals. Once we experience this selfishness our task is to raise it up to a higher expression. Then we experience ourselves as independent, highly self-aware, individuals. The highest expression of the human 'I' is referred to in the bible as *ego eimi* – I AM. Full awareness of our I AM is to have full self consciousness.

As we become aware of the activity of the 'I' the third part of our being, our spirit, comes to life. This is referred to as *pneuma*. The three activities of our spirit are Imagination, Inspiration and Intuition. We have experiences of these functions when we are able to raise our feeling, thinking and willing to a higher expression through a conscious connection with our 'I'.

1. BLESSED ARE THE POOR IN SPIRIT, FOR THEIRS IS THE KINGDOM OF HEAVEN. MT 5:3

One: Recognising our I AM

The only Gospel to set out the nine Beatitudes from the Sermon on the Mount is St. Matthew's Gospel. Surely they must be mentioned in St John's Gospel in a less obvious way. The purpose of the Beatitudes is to show us how to connect our I AM to the nine members of our being; Physical body, etheric, astral, three soul regions and three spiritual regions. Since the Gospel of St John also reveals how we connect with our I AM and Christ, John must speak about the Beatitudes differently. Over the next nine months we can explore the possible texts in St John's Gospel that give us deeper insight into the Beatitude process.

Blessed, *makarios*, is said to mean happiness. Happiness can only truly be experienced if placed in contrast to its opposite; sadness or sorrow. To be blessed must mean more than happiness. In fact, in the Beatitudes, blessed points to a state of being that appears to be exactly the opposite of common understanding. Isn't rich in spirit better then poor in spirit? We could say that to be blessed is to be Christened. So does it make sense to say, "Christened are the poor in spirit, for theirs is the kingdom of heaven?"

Who are people poor in spirit? Could they be people who can't decide what to do? People who are at a crossroads in their life? They are empty of ideas about the next steps to take? When such a person is around us we immediately want to fill their void by giving them advice; we think that our advice will enrich them. In this way we think that we are giving to the poor. Yet the person who resists receiving our alms, and calls on their own inner resources to make a decision - without outside help - will be strong and courageous. They will stand in their inheritance, in their kingdom, as self-made beings. They are the self-born ones. They engage their I AM in the depths of their being and make decisions in tune with their destiny.

The spirit, *pneumati*, that people sought at the time of Christ was outside them; to be found in the medium, the clairvoyant, the gods which provided guidance from outside. The need for outside guidance ceased when Christ came because he gave us direct access to our own I AM, our own inner guidance. We must no longer use any forms of divination to assist us to make choices.

Our task is to connect up with our I AM. Our I AM writes the blueprint for our incarnations. Our I AM decides which karmic situations need balancing in each of our earthly lives. Our I AM places us in the right country with the right family and friends (or enemies). John records the proof of this in chapter nine.

And his disciples asked him, "Rabbi, who sinned, this man or his parents, that he was born blind?" Jesus answered, "It was not that this man sinned, or his parents, but that the works of God might be made manifest in him. Jn 9:2-3

If we accept that we are poor in spirit, that our connection with our I AM is weak, and we resolve to strengthen it, we will step into the kingdom of heaven *"that the works of God might be made manifest in us."* Being poor in spirit is certainly found in our ability to accept that we are blind.

What do we do when meet someone who is blind? Do we think, "Poor person, I wish I could heal you?" If so, then we want to interfere with that person's opportunity to connect up with their I AM. At the same time, are we aware that the blind person experiences our thoughts of wanting them to see like us? What effect would this have on them? They would immediately feel inferior, poor. In this way we inflict our opinions silently on others.

The first Beatitude is telling us that the person in the inferior position is actually superior. They have the greatest opportunity of all, by accepting their poverty, by not fighting it. It is in these circumstances that their I AM can shine into their physical body and spiritualise it. When we accept that we are poor in spirit, immediately the gross matter of our body becomes lighter. Then the forces of soul and spirit can move more freely throughout our being and we experience heaven on earth.

When we don't accept the situations that present themselves in our lives, when we wish we were more fortunate, less troubled, less poor and so on, we are really signalling to our I AM that we cannot co-operate with its plan. We want to blame our parents or our bad karma and we are blind to our opportunities, rejecting our poverty. All the while, the etheric Christ stands before us longing to be seen; longing for us to accept our inheritance; longing for us to have the kingdom of heaven in our lives now.

Two: *Allowing ideas to flow like respiration*

Spirit, *pneumati*, could also be translated 'breath'. We are air-breathing beings but that is not all that we 'breathe' in. Images, ideas, and concepts flow into us and out from us continually. In fact it is important for the health of our soul to allow these things to enter into us and then to express ourselves out into the world again. The more rhythmic this process is the better.

What tends to happen, however, is that we either prevent some things entering in, or we suppress our outward expression. A type of hoarding takes place; we collect things outside us that we don't want to enter into us, and we collect things inside us that we don't want to express outwardly. The decision to do this rests entirely on our opinions.

Opinions rule society today. We all have opinions about what is good and what is bad and it closes us off, it restricts our soul-breathing. We could say that we are rich in the spirit of our opinions. Unless we become poor in this spirit of opinions ours will never be the kingdom of heaven.

There are many examples of this in St John's Gospel but none as powerful as those found in chapter 19. *The Jews answered him [Pilate], "We have a law, and by that law he ought to die, because he has made himself the Son of God." ....Upon this Pilate sought to release him, but the Jews cried out, "If you release this man, you are not Caesar's friend; every one who makes himself a king sets himself against Caesar."* Jn 19:7 & 12

To the Jews, the idea that a human being could be the Son of God was unacceptable. The idea that we must be Caesar's friend was acceptable. The Jews prevented the first idea from entering into their soul; the second idea was firmly planted in their soul, never to be released. Both situations meant that the kingdom of heaven could not be theirs.

It is crucial today, more than ever, that we remain open to ideas as well as replacing some of the ideas that we have. We may feel insecure when we don't stand on the foundation of our opinions but unless we embrace new ideas, new possibilities, the kingdom of heaven will be out of reach.

Every time we tell someone that we don't agree with them, we scourge them, and place a crown of thorns on them. When we reject their ideas they are in agony. Their ideas could well be from the kingdom of heaven. They may have made themselves poor in spirit so that they could receive new ideas, but unless these ideas agree with ours we cry, *"Away with him, away with him, crucify him!"*

Our soul desperately needs harmony, that rhythmic harmony that comes from breathing in, holding briefly, and breathing out. This soul-harmony must be self-created; it is no longer God given. We must develop the courage to take in the ideas of others, look at them, and breathe them out. We can only do this by being objective; we cannot do it out of sympathy and antipathy. By looking at everything, and comparing everything, and then letting it go, we will be left with the essence of truth. It is like panning for gold.

To be poor in spirit is to stop thinking that our ideas are the right ideas. The more people we can share our ideas with, while at the same time taking in their ideas, the closer we will come to the truth that sets us free. The more we impose our ideas on others, the more we express our likes and dislikes, the more division we create echoing the words of the Jews, *"We have a law!"*

Further to this, consciousness evolves, ideas always need further development. We acknowledge this in our language by saying, "This is an idea whose time has come." The healthy soul always has new ideas which are waiting for their time to come.

Another danger lies in the half-formed idea. This is when we grasp at an understanding before the idea has fully developed. We need the strong and pure will of the I AM to develop ideas fully, to see the gold in them. The half-formed idea is always open to manipulation and can be adopted as a generalised opinion which is not personally thought through. This happens in our soul when our feelings prompt us to take a shortcut. Yet, it is only through our courageous will that we find the kingdom of heaven.

In our willingness to empty ourselves of old ideas and partial ideas, to breathe them out and breathe in new ideas, we will experience the kingdom of heaven as a place where we can observe all manner of possibilities. Then we will be blessed, Christened.

Three: Experience eternity in the present

What is the kingdom of heaven? St Matthew has quite a lot to say about this kingdom. *"Repent, for the kingdom of heaven is at hand."* Mt 3:2 *"sit at table with Abraham, Isaac, and Jacob in the kingdom of heaven.* Mt 8:11 *The kingdom of heaven has suffered violence, and men of violence take it by force.* Mt 11:12 *The kingdom of heaven may be compared to a man who sowed good seed in his field;* or *it is like a grain of mustard seed;* or *like leaven which a woman took and hid in three measures of flour;* or *like treasure hidden in a field;* or *like a merchant in search of fine pearls;* or *like a net which was thrown into the sea and gathered fish of every kind;* Mt 13

St John refers to the Kingdom of God twice in relation to Nicodemus and when he speaks of heaven it is in terms of the I AM: *"I am the living bread which came down from heaven;"* 6:51 and *"This is the bread which came down from heaven, ... he who eats this bread will live for ever."* Jn 6:58

So what can the kingdom of heaven be? It is at hand; it is with the patriarchs of the race that gave birth to the vehicle for the Cosmic Christ; it has suffered violence; it is like a seed or the sowing of a seed; it is like hidden leaven or hidden treasure; and it is like a searching merchant or even a fishing net.

The Gospel writers are telling us that the kingdom of heaven is a mystery process which we can identify if we read the occult script (the hidden messages) in the world around us. They are also alerting us to the fact that this process is going on in our being. We can become aware of this process if we are poor in spirit, if we dare to empty ourselves.

John gives us a real clue to this process when he says that [the] I AM [is] the bread if life, if we eat it we will - not live forever – but, we will live in eternity, now, here on earth. What is it like in eternity? Time and space are experienced differently.

To understand how time and space can be experienced differently we need to become aware of how we experience them now. Usually we don't have enough of them – how often do we say, "Give me more time," or "Give me some space"? This feeling of needing more time and space is directly related to our consciousness. For the most part we are conscious of being separated from everything and everyone, including our own I AM. This separation gives us a feeling of being limited. Eternity does the opposite.

Eternity can be described as true space. It can also be described as living time. This is the real power of 'now'. If we can find a way to live in eternity then we will cease to experience the limits of our earthly consciousness. In eternity, past, present and future can be weighted equally in our consciousness. The pressure of time and space is removed and we have a sense of being able to do all things in him who strengthens us, as St Paul reminds the Philippians.

Our ability to experience eternity is directly linked to how conscious we are. Being conscious, is, of course, the sole purpose of our life. We must admit, however, that this is a most difficult task. It takes an enormous amount of will to remember everything that happened today, let alone every day of our lives so far. Rarely are we even conscious of the present moment because past memories often crowd into the present. It is virtually impossible to be conscious of the future – at least with our earthly mind.

In the kingdom of heaven, where we experience eternity, we are able to participate in the resurrection forces which are directly related to our ability to connect up with our I AM. Many of the descriptions in Matthew's Gospel are images of the resurrection forces; the seeds, the leaven, the hidden treasure, the fishing.

In the kingdom of heaven we can also be in the presence of mighty beings like Abraham, Isaac, and Jacob who prepared the way for us to connect with our I AM.

In eternity, with access to the resurrection forces, we are enabled to experience the Mystery of Golgotha in our own being and claim the kingdom of heaven in our lives, now. No matter what war, what terror, what misfortune – large or small – we see the big picture.

Rudolf Steiner puts this beautifully in the Fifth Gospel, "Out of suffering was born the all abiding cosmic love which went through the moment of highest divine impotence in order to give birth to that impulse which we know as the Christ-Impulse." Indeed, Christened are the poor in spirit, for theirs is the kingdom of heaven.

Four: Balance material and physical

We can look at each of the nine Beatitudes in terms of the Christ-ening of the nine parts of our being; physical, etheric, astral and then the three soul and three spiritual regions. If we apply the first Beatitude to our physical body we will find clues about how our I AM is enlivened in our body.

Our physical body is the most fully developed part of us. The physiology of the human being is a marvel. The way our skeleton, muscles and skin hold and protect our organs in a life giving way is truly wondrous.

For the most part we think that the physical body is all there is of us. Even if we have studied otherwise, it is still very difficult for us to think of our body merely as a vehicle for our soul and spirit. Every day we do things that benefit our body at the expense of our soul and spirit. This is natural because we live in the age of the "poor in spirit". Our bodily consciousness blocks out our soul and spirit.

Even when we study the spiritual teachings it is very easy to interpret them materialistically. In fact, very often we don't understand spiritual teachings because we mistakenly place them in a physical context. Or we even expect to see spiritual things in a material form. Thomas reveals how this can happen.

Then he said to Thomas, "Put your finger here, and see my hands; and put out your hand, and place it in my side; do not be faithless, but believing." Thomas answered him, "My Lord and my God!" Jesus said to him, "Have you believed because you have seen me? Blessed are those who have not seen and yet believe." Jn 20:27-29

What is this telling us? How it is possible for us to believe that which we haven't seen? We use the underlying force of our physical body, our will, to make ourselves believe. When we do this a fundamental change happens in our soul. It awakens and becomes conscious of our spirit that gives us firsthand knowledge.

Until then, we accept that we are blind and begging, and we say, "I know that I have an I AM. I know that it has planned my incarnation, set up all the opportunities and the obstacles, and even though I am not fully conscious of these, I will believe that there is a plan." How hard is it to let go and allow this plan to be carried out? Don't we always want to interfere? We want to take control, to feel powerful and ward off any feeling of powerlessness?

The poor are the ones who beg, they are the ones who can swallow their pride and experience powerlessness. Then, the I AM will come and we will see through its eyes. This is the story of the healing of the blind man in John 9. *The neighbors and those who had seen him before as a beggar, said, "Is not this the man who used to sit and beg?" Some said, "It is he"; others said, "No, but he is like him." He said, "I am (the man —these words have been added)."* Jn 9:8-9

If we faithfully examine ourselves we will discover that the wellbeing of our body is a selfish thing, we are so inclined to put ourselves first. Observe children; it is unusual if they don't want to be first, to have the largest glass of juice or the bag with the most lollies. Our natural, unawakened soul is inclined to do the same, instincts outweigh reason. Our spirit, especially our I AM, is never interested in being first or taking advantage of others, it always experiences what the other person experiences. In the kingdom of heaven competition is replaced by a kind of spiritual strategy which works for the common good.

Our greatest challenge, while we work to spiritualise our consciousness, is to balance the physical with the spiritual. Usually we are either too physical or too spiritual. So, balanced are the poor in spirit. Those who are balanced, who have one foot in the physical world and one in the spiritual world, have the consciousness of the kingdom of heaven.

This is what St Matthew means when he says, *Again I tell you, it is easier for a camel to go through the eye of a needle than for a rich man to enter the kingdom of God."* Mt 19:24 When we over-value money and influence we are magnetised to the earth and what it has to offer. This means that we lose the balance, the blessedness, which gives us access to the kingdom of heaven where we are truly rich.

This balance means that we experience great compassion for those who cannot achieve the same balance as we do. We don't criticise or judge those who do not live in the kingdom of heavenly consciousness. We simply love them because we know that the spirit of Christ is within them and always has the potential to shine.

Five: See Jesus the resister rather than Judas the betrayer

This Greek word used here for poor is *ptochoi* and it gives a sense of begging. *Penichros* is the other word for poor which speaks more about being needy. So *ptochoi*-poor indicates that the person is taking some action. They swallow their pride and actually admit that they are poor and then have the courage to openly ask for assistance. *Penichros*-poor is more about surreptitiously seeking attention to boost our self-esteem.

Even though we could regard begging as a parasitical action, the beggar in spirit is the one who has actually begun connecting with their I AM. They accept how poor they are and realise that they are cut off from wisdom and truth. They do not bluff by making out that they know who they are and what life is all about. The poor in spirit freely admit that they do not have the necessary self-knowledge that is required by those who will be self-born, self-generated.

If we look at the story of Mary anointing Jesus' feet in John 12 we can come to understand something more about those who are *potchoi*-poor. In this story Judas can represent the adversary which is always with us. Always trying to distract us and steal our energy, making it more difficult for us to give birth to our True Self.

Mary took a pound of costly ointment of pure nard and anointed the feet of Jesus and wiped his feet with her hair; and the house was filled with the fragrance of the ointment. But Judas Iscariot, one of his disciples (he who was to betray him), said, "Why was this ointment not sold for three hundred denarii and given to the poor?" This he said, not that he cared for the poor but because he was a thief, and as he had the money box he used to take what was put into it. Jesus said, "Let her alone, let her keep it for the day of my burial. The poor you always have with you, but you do not always have me." Jn 12:3-8

Of course Judas doesn't care for the poor. He is trying to thwart their efforts to make the kingdom of heaven their own. He doesn't want the anointing to happen; anointing which is an essential part of the process of connecting up with our I AM. Nor does he care about the poor (in spirit) – those who acknowledge that they are cut off from spiritual worlds and strive to reconnect.

Judas's purpose is to provide that opposition which prompts

our striving. By striving to resist him we strengthen ourselves. We use our own energy to improve our situation – even if it means begging; at least we are taking action.

Shouldn't we look, not to Judas the betrayer but rather to Jesus who endures the betrayal? Jesus, the I AM, is conscious; the closer he gets to the cross the more conscious he is. He is aware of the motives of Judas who seeks every opportunity to distract and disturb. We too must become so conscious that we don't waste our time and energy by kicking and screaming about things that are actually opportunities for us to know ourselves more fully.

Notice that Jesus, too, seems to be quite dismissive of the poor. However, he would have known that once he accomplished his mission, the full connection with the Cosmic I AM, the Cosmic Christ, that there would be many beggars for this spiritual gift that he was making available to all human beings. He is the forerunner as Paul tells the Hebrews: ... *we who have fled for refuge might have strong encouragement to seize the hope set before us. We have this as a sure and steadfast anchor of the soul, a hope that enters into the inner shrine behind the curtain, where Jesus has gone as a forerunner on our behalf* ... Hb 6:18-19

There is an insecurity that accompanies the poor in spirit. How much of our energy do we squander in our efforts to feel secure? Judas took the money in the money box, the energy that people gave, so that he could feel more secure. Our security doesn't come from taking energy from others; security can only come by looking to the forerunner. The experiences of Jesus, especially in the Gospel of St John, the I AM Gospel, show us the way. If we can find the courage to live with our insecurity, if we resist being needy and take action to become poor (beggars) in spirit, the kingdom of heaven will be ours.

If we resist being negative about all the difficulties that are an inherent part of our lives, if we see Jesus the resister rather than Judas the betrayer, then we will live in this consciousness that is the kingdom of heaven. This kingdom is the place where we truly know ourselves. Here we can experience that we are threefold beings of body, soul and spirit taking part in a planned evolution. For now, all we need to do is to dare to be poor in spirit!

2. BLESSED ARE THOSE WHO MOURN, FOR THEY WILL BE COMFORTED. MT 5:4

One: The challenges of self-responsibility

To mourn is to be sorrowful because something has been taken away from us. As we evolve as human beings something is always being taken away and something new is added. If we look at human development just in the last 100 years we can see that the horse as a means of transport has been taken away and replaced by motor vehicles. The need to produce our own food has been taken away and the supermarket (and McDonalds) has been added to our lives.

If we look at this in terms of the cosmos and the spiritual beings who guide the human race we can also see that some things are taken away and other things are added. Before Golgotha we were connected to our I AM through Jehovah. Then, our I AM could be described as a group spirit. Now, the group spirit has been individualised and we each have access to our own human spirit, our own I AM. So Jehovah has been taken away and Christ has been added to our lives. This was the cause of much sorrow among the people at the time of Christ – and still is today.

Jehovah was the god outside us who guided us with external laws. Christ is the god inside us making us self-regulating and self-responsible. During this transition we are often filled with sorrow for what we have lost, especially when it isn't clear what has been added. Also, there is a certain sense of security in placing things outside of us. Taking personal responsibility can be uncomfortable and often arduous.

Blessed, Christened, are those who mourn for the loss of outside assistance. In our sorrow we realise that we have to find the assistance inside, from our own resources. We have to look inside for the connection to Christ and the I AM he gifted us. This is not easy, the method is not clear. We have to strive to discover the rules ourselves before we can follow them. St. John is a good place to look for hints, obscure though they can be at times. Jesus talks to his disciples about this sorrow, this mourning, in chapter 16.

"I have said all this to you to keep you from falling away. They will put you out of the synagogues; indeed, the hour is coming when whoever kills you will think he is offering service to God. And they will do this because they have not known the Father, nor me. But I have said these things to you, that when their hour comes you may remember that I told you of them. "I did not say these things to you from the beginning, because I was with you. But now I am going to him who sent me; yet none of you asks me, 'Where are you going?' But because I have said these things to you, sorrow has filled your hearts. Nevertheless I tell you the truth: it is to your advantage that I go away, for if I do not go away, the Comforter will not come to you; but if I go, I will send him to you. Jn 16:1-7

Because the second Beatitude speaks about the changes in our etheric body we can ask, what is being taken away and what is being added? For the disciples, the physical presence of Christ was taken away and his etheric presence was added. That's "where he was going". For us, our etheric body is loosening and we begin to lose the security of our physical existence because our etheric life is being added - rekindled. This is very painful because the world doesn't accept us. It wants to kill our new understanding of the etheric presence of Christ.

However, the more we look towards the etheric Christ, the more we can mourn the loss of our secure physical outlook, then we will be comforted. The comforter, *parakletos*, is the Holy Spirit. As Christ unites with our "I" he doesn't make it a clone of him, he fills our "I" with the Holy Spirit so that our sorrow can be soothed. But first we must experience the sorrow before we can experience the comfort. Yet, so often the sorrow is too painful that we seek our own comfort ahead of the Holy Comforter.

What we don't realise is, that as we work on our spiritual development, which softens our etheric body, we become painfully aware of our spiritual shortcomings. Then we promptly douse the pain with something comforting, something physically pleasurable. So it's a catch twenty-two situation. The softer our etheric, the more we remember, and the more we remember, the more we want to forget. We want to remove the sorrow, stop the mourning and continue in our unconscious ways. When we feel the pain of something being taken away we need to have the strength to wait for the Comforter. We must also bear the pain quietly and calmly; showing our tears to God and our smile to the world.

Two: Through mourning we experience immortality

The quintessential mourner in St. John's Gospel is Mary Magdalene. She was the first to arrive at the tomb to discover that Jesus' body was no longer there. Undoubtedly, her purpose for going to the tomb was to mourn, to immerse herself in the sorrow of her loss.

Is this what mourning is? Experiencing pain because the one we loved has been removed from us? Is mourning about us? or is mourning about assisting the one who has died by remembering and honouring their life? After all, they have simply moved into another dimension of consciousness, they are still with us. So mourning can be a time when we realise what we have gained rather than what we think we may have lost. Mourning can then be a period of adjustment while we get used to a new working relationship with the person who has simply stepped out of their physical body and taken up their spiritual body. What a comforting idea that is.

John tells the story this way: *But Mary stood weeping outside the tomb, and as she wept she stooped to look into the tomb; and she saw two angels in white, sitting where the body of Jesus had lain, one at the head and one at the feet. They said to her, "Woman, why are you weeping?" She said to them, "Because they have taken away my Lord, and I do not know where they have laid him." Saying this, she turned round and saw Jesus standing, but she did not know that it was Jesus. Jesus said to her, "Woman, why are you weeping? Whom do you seek?" Supposing him to be the gardener, she said to him, "Sir, if you have carried him away, tell me where you have laid him, and I will take him away." Jesus said to her, "Mary." She turned and said to him in Hebrew, "Rab-bo'ni!" (which means Teacher).* Jn 20:11-16

The story is a great example of how our earthly consciousness continually faces the unexpected when it looks into spiritual matters. Even though Mary clearly has spiritual perception - she sees and hears angels as well as the risen Christ - she also makes a series of errors. We too make these errors when we interpret spirit materialistically. In our present period of evolution a new kind of spiritual perception is awakening in us. To develop it more we need to use our thinking to 'see' spirit. We must tell ourselves that those who have died, especially those who have developed their spiritual consciousness while they were in the body, are with us after death, but in a different 'dimension'. Then we will be comforted.

Mourning is sometimes referred to as pining. We pine for what we have lost. Now, the pine tree is an evergreen tree and it symbolises immortality. Immortality is nothing more than bridging life and death – seeing them as a continuation but with different conditions of consciousness. When we experience our loved ones around us after they have left their body we continue to work together. We no longer look for their body and we see them 'standing' there.

Notice, also, the reference to Mary turning, it is used twice. John wouldn't use this word if he wasn't pointing to something. Why would she turn a second time, she had already turned away from the angels and towards Jesus standing (supposing him to be the gardener)? Is John saying that Mary is turning her attention from one thing to another? - from the tomb, which represents our body, to the spiritual reality of the risen Christ.

Think about Mary Magdalene for a moment. She can represent our soul which used to be drawn to the pleasures of earth and then discovers the pleasures of heaven. Physical love transformed into agape - love without boundaries. The depth of her love is the reason that she is the first one to see the resurrected, Christened-Jesus. Her ability to turn her attention to both worlds, the spiritual world and the physical world, is because of the depth of her love. We too must develop this depth of love so that we can stand in both worlds equally. This will be our only comfort. As long as we cannot experience immortality we will not be comforted. When we experience immortality our sorrows lose their significance in the scheme of things.

As soon as we experience immortality we see Jesus standing there, Jesus, the perfect human united with the great sun-spirit, Christ. He will be our Rabboni and teach us more about the secrets of immortality. He will show us how to live in our physical body and at the same time experience the spiritual worlds, but only after we have experienced the sorrow; after we have experienced the limitation of our modern consciousness.

Three: Resurrection of consciousness

The death of Lazarus places another powerful picture of mourning before us. Mary, Martha and the Jews weep for their loss. What have they lost actually? Is it just that their brother and friend has died? Or is it that life as they have known it has come to an end? Rudolf Steiner says that Jesus wept for joy because of this situation.

...and many of the Jews had come to Martha and Mary to console them concerning their brother. When Martha heard that Jesus was coming, she went and met him, while Mary sat in the house. Martha said to Jesus, "Lord, if you had been here, my brother would not have died. And even now I know that whatever you ask from God, God will give you." Jesus said to her, "Your brother will rise again."

... When Jesus saw her weeping, and the Jews who came with her also weeping, he was deeply moved in spirit and troubled; and he said, "Where have you laid him?" They said to him, "Lord, come and see." Jesus wept. So the Jews said, "See how he loved him!" But some of them said, "Could not he who opened the eyes of the blind man have kept this man from dying?" Jn 11:19-23 and 33-37

Our whole being is experiencing a process of transformation. More than at any other time in the evolution of mankind we are being transformed. Essentially, all that is physical in us is being spiritualised. We have been deeply embedded in the physical world and its sensory processes and now we must return to the spiritual worlds, this time as self-born individuals. The speed with which this happens is entirely up to us.

The focal point of this transformation is our consciousness. Jesus will not keep our earth-bound consciousness from dying, not under any circumstances. He wants it to die and to resurrect in a higher way. All those ideas that constitute our consciousness have to die. They have to be laid aside. They served us well while we conducted our ordinary earthly affairs, but now that we are connecting up with our I AM, and the Christ impulse is enlivening us, we must enter into a period of mourning. During this period we have the opportunity to recognise that many of the ideas that we have developed during our life are no longer useful. At the same time we realise that we have yet to become fully aware of our new spiritualised consciousness.

How does the death of Lazarus speak of this? Death is a process where our life-giving forces disconnect from our physical body. A death where we don't really die, like Lazarus here, means that our life-giving forces, our etheric forces, are raised up, spiritualised. Now, a key factor to consider is that our memories lie within these etheric forces. But when the etheric forces are spiritualised we no longer need our earthly memories because through inspiration we can tap into cosmic memory, we can inspire them, breathe them in. These universal memories contain everything that we have ever experienced, in this life and all previous lives. Imagine tapping into the memory of past lives and grieving for the people and events of those times that are no longer part of us.

Of course we can't do this until we have control of our emotions. We can't see these past events if we are going to weep and wail for what we have lost. We have to learn to bear the sorrow with equanimity. It is the kind of composure that comes from being able to equally accept a 'yes' or a 'no' about something that really matters to us. Like Martha was challenged to accept that 'no' from Jesus when he didn't drop everything to come and heal Lazarus.

We need this same composure when we form our opinions. Mostly we are swayed by our likes and dislikes. Nothing works against our developing spiritual consciousness more than being swayed by sympathy and antipathy, by approval or aversion. In everything we face in life we need equanimity. Observe how many times a day we say, "I like that," or "I don't like them." We are echoing the Jews who said, *"Could not he who opened the eyes of the blind man have kept this man from dying?"*

When we do this we deny ourselves the opportunity to mourn, as well as the opportunity to be comforted. During this period we do not need opinions, no matter how well thought through they are, we need to have conversations with other like-minded people so that we can stretch and shape our ideas into a new spiritual form. It isn't about deciding who should heal whom; it is about creating the space for Christ to transform our consciousness.

Four: The Holy Spirit

During this week we celebrate the festival of Michaelmas. Archangel Michael is said to be part of the Holy Spirit, part of the comforter. Michael is also said to be the countenance of Christ. How can we know whether these statements are true? Only if we test them, only if we think about them and try to experience the presence and purpose of the Archangel Michael in our lives.

Understanding esoteric truth is a crucial task today if we are to become conscious of our I AM. Becoming conscious of our I AM means that we experience life from that perspective of consciousness which is different from our everyday consciousness. Understanding esoteric truth is not a complex academic exercise. In fact, esoteric truth, in its simplest form, can be seen everywhere in our lives ... if we look. At first, armed with a few esoteric facts, we can begin to think them into daily events. Quite soon after that our consciousness will begin to change. We will view life differently and many difficulties in our life will be transformed by the I AM viewpoint.

In the search to find this second Beatitude in St John's Gospel we find several references to the comforter or counselor as the Revised Standard Version translates it. In John 14 Jesus says, *But the Counselor,* [the comforter - *parakletos*] *the Holy Spirit, whom the Father will send in my name, he will teach you all things, and bring to your remembrance all that I have said to you.* Jn 14:26

Now obviously we can't remember 'all that Jesus said to us' because we weren't there! But, that is not what Jesus is actually saying. He is saying that with the aid of this Holy Spirit we will remember all things that our "I" – *ego* in the Greek – tells us. So when we become conscious of our I AM, then we can hear about ourselves, that unknown part of ourselves that is obscured by today's consciousness. Of course, this unknown part of us is the part that has experienced all our past lives. We will sure need the comforter when we get to the stage of becoming conscious of our past lives.

Another thing to realise is that comfort would never come to those who are content, those who are full of content [kon-tent].

We have to experience the emptiness; we have to grieve for our losses before we can experience the comforter.

In Chapter 15 John reports Jesus saying: *But when the Counselor* (comforter) *comes, whom I shall send to you from the Father, even the Spirit of truth, who proceeds from the Father, he will bear witness to me;* Jn 15:26

Here is the mystery of the Trinity; the Father, Son and Holy Spirit. How do we make sense of this? Even though they are the three in one, they each have a different role to play. Chapters 14, 15 and 16 in John's Gospel make a lot more sense if we are able to understand something of the different roles they each play.

A lecture Rudolf Steiner delivered on July 30, 1922 sheds quite a lot of light on the mystery of the Trinity. Before Christ, when a person was initiated, the Father entered into them and made them conscious of their "I". This happened ahead of the rest of the population and foreshadowed the future. Christ came to make it possible for everyone, in the natural course of events, to become conscious of their "I", to be self-conscious. At that time, those who had spiritual sight could see the difference between those who were made conscious of their "I" 'artificially' through the Father, and Jesus who bore the radiance of the Holy Spirit, symbolised by the dove at his baptism.

We might wonder why, if Christ came once and for all, we have to work so hard to become conscious of our "I" and integrate Christ into our being. Remember it took Jesus over three years to fully absorb the Christ spirit, and many lifetimes before that to become conscious of his "I". If Christ had entered into human beings as a matter of course, without any effort from us, then we would be clones of him. He would obscure our consciousness and we would not be able to become conscious of our own "I". Therefore he would obliterate all that we had become up till now and we would become part of the homogenous, undifferentiated universe from whence we came. What is the point of that? Why didn't we just stay put in the beginning?

To prevent this from happening, Christ has to go away, we have to mourn and then he can send the comforter so that we can strive to become conscious through our own effort. This is what John is telling us in Ch 16. *Nevertheless I tell you the truth: it is to your advantage that I go away, for if I do not go away, the Counselor* (comforter) *will not come to you; but if I go, I will send him to you.* Jn 16:7

So we could say that the Father worked in the past, the Spirit works in the present and Christ will work in the future when we have prepared ourselves to receive him fully into ourselves. In John 14 Jesus says, *"If you love me, you will keep my commandments. And I will pray the Father, and he will give you another Counselor,* (comforter) *to be with you for ever, even the Spirit of truth, whom the world cannot receive, because it neither sees him nor knows him; you know him, for he dwells with you, and will be in you.* Jn 14:15-17

Who dwells with us, and will be in us? Our I AM! How could this comforter be with us forever? It could if it was something that we created, something that becomes part of us. A Holy Spirit comes into being when we put effort into understanding esoteric truth. When we awaken our soul and become conscious of our thinking instead of aimlessly allowing thoughts to flow through our mind. Archangel Michael has thrown the dragon down into our midst and we must be vigilant. If we don't work with these esoteric thoughts then Ahrimanic beings take over our thoughts, they think in us because we don't stake the claim in our mind. If that is not incentive to become as conscious as possible then what is?

A Holy Spirit also dwells in us when we love one another, respect one another, uplift one another and honour the freedom each other. Every time we truly stand in the shoes of the other person, when we feel their joy or their sorrow as if it were our own, we create that Holy Spirit, that comforter who will be with us forever. This is the spirit of Michaelmas which we can experience in its intensity at this time of the year. It is the spirit of Michael that carries us through to Christmas when Christ can be born in us anew.

3. BLESSED ARE THE MEEK, FOR THEY SHALL INHERIT THE EARTH. MT 5:5

One: Preventing our astral from displacing our I AM

If the Beatitudes are to assist us to become conscious of our I AM and to allow Christ to pulse through our being then we need some strong images of what actually takes place within us. What do we imagine happens within our being when we become conscious of our I AM? What exactly do we experience when we become conscious of the influence of Christ in our being?

Esoteric knowledge gives us all sorts of terminology with which to express this but nothing is more powerful than a living picture which lights up our soul. The most powerful picture is the one we create ourselves.

For instance, in our imagination we can create a picture of our soul that is full of many images streaming through us; containing everything that we see and experience and everything stored in our memory. This stream can bubble along evenly or it can become a torrent. The speed of the stream is directly related to our response to life's events. Some of the images from these responses are helpful and some are not. Primarily it is our feelings which affect the flow of the water.

In this stream are islands of thought. They allow us to step out of the flowing impulses and images for awhile. Then we can make sense of these images. If our thinking is not constructive then the stream, propelled by feelings, will rise up and wash us off the island. Sometimes we can use our will to affect the way the stream flows, but if we erect a barrier - perhaps blocking an incident that we don't want to face - the water will simply find a different course.

By allowing images like this live in our soul, our soul comes to life, it awakens from its natural dreamy state. The result is that we then become more conscious of our I AM and the presence of Christ. In this awakened state our self-knowledge increases and we know what it means to be meek.

The word 'meek' does not imply weakness. Meek is not about the way we express ourselves outwardly, but rather about the gentleness and grace within us. It speaks of a person expressing themselves through their higher self instead of their lower, unrefined astral. Self interest is raised to an experience of brotherhood, of fraternity.

A powerful picture of meekness and fraternity can be found in John 4 where John records Jesus' picture of harvesting what others have laboured for.

Do you not say, 'Four months more and then the harvest'? I tell you, open your eyes and look at the fields! They are ripe for harvest. Even now the reaper draws his wages, even now he harvests the crop for eternal life, so that the sower and the reaper may be glad together. Thus the saying 'One sows and another reaps' is true. I sent you to reap what you have not worked for. Others have done the hard work, and you have reaped the benefits of their labor." Jn 4:35-38

This notion of someone else reaping the benefits of someone's hard work does not sit well in today's consciousness. We want to reap the benefits of our own hard labour. We also want to do things for ourselves, in our own way; we don't want others to do things for us. Therefore we are not meek. This is one of the difficulties of becoming conscious of our I AM, we want to over-emphasise our individuality, expressing it in the world instead of treasuring it within us.

Thus the saying 'One sows and another reaps' speaks to us of the true community we will experience when our astral is refined in the fire of our I AM. This third Beatitude is about cleansing our astral. Our passions, desires and emotions are refined so that our astral becomes our tool and does not masquerade as our Real Self. We gently and graciously work so that others may reap; and we enjoy the fruits of the labour of those who came before us. This is the experience of those who are strongly connected to their I AM and conscious of the presence of Christ in their being. The harvest is to be conscious.

Inheriting the earth points to this part of evolution where we develop our connection with our I AM. The last cycle of evolution was about developing our connection with our astral. Now that we are connected with our astral we can prepare it to receive the "I" which in its highest expression is the I AM. When we become conscious of the esoteric reality of this earth, conscious of the presence of the spiritual worlds and its beings in and around us, we will inherit the earth. Then we become at one with the body of Christ who claimed this earth as his body when his blood flowed from the cross at Golgotha. The inheritance of the earth is the I AM which we can only receive if we are meek.

Two: Karma unites our lower and higher self

When we inherit the earth we receive our birth-right. Our birth-right is the I AM and our task is to become conscious of it. This birth-right is not a given. There is always the chance of being disinherited. In order to avoid being disinherited we must prove ourselves worthy.

The process of proving that we are worthy means that we have to become more aware of who we really are. While we are only conscious of our immediate physical surroundings we can say that we operate out of our small "i". This small "i" is a mirrored-reflection of our I AM, our true spiritual being. This Real or True Self, our I AM, is using the earth as a proving ground. In a way it is bizarre. We have been split in two and we have to be rejoined, but joined differently. Our two 'personalities', the higher and the lower, are trying to find each other so that we can feel whole. We could also say that we are two different consciousnesses trying to become one consciousness. This has to happen through our own effort. It is not bestowed on us by the gods, by the beings of the Spiritual Hierarchy.

This whole-making process does not happen by having good thoughts or refined feelings. It can only happen through our actions, through our deeds. Our Real Self reveals itself to our earthly consciousness through the way we act in the world, through our tendencies and our talents. We can think all the nice thoughts in the world but if we then act badly towards someone we steer a course towards being disinherited.

The agency that unites these two 'expressions' of self is karma. It is through karma that we can prove that we are worthy of the inheritance. All the situations we face in our life are prepared by our I AM who has planned for us to engage with them and resolve them. Karma is all about balance, one action balanced by another. It can be likened to climbing a ladder. It isn't until we bear our weight evenly on one foot that we can make the next move to a higher rung. This ladder leads us to full union with our I AM.

Therefore, it is mandatory that we meet each event in our lives with meekness. We must strive to meet even the most difficult situations in our life with gentleness and graciousness, not just appearing gentle and gracious on the outside but having a real experience of gentleness and graciousness within.

Our lives are like a plant growing from seed to flower which then produces the seed for our next incarnation. Plants are the epitome of meekness. In all weather they do not deviate from the path of producing the seed to ensure the survival of the species.

So, each life we must weather the storms of karma so that we produce a strong seed and work our way towards receiving our birth-right. On June 5, 1911 Rudolf Steiner spoke these powerful words about karma. *We may meet a person who mocks or even insults us. If we have immersed ourselves in the teaching of reincarnation and karma for a long time, we will wonder who has spoken the hurtful, insulting words our ears have heard. Who has heaped mockery upon us – or even who has raised the hand to hit us? We will then realize that we ourselves did this. The hand raised for the blow only appears to belong to the other person. Ultimately, we cause the other to raise his or her hand against us through our own past karma.* Appendix: Spiritual Guidance of the Individual and Humanity.

This quote brings to mind the mocking in John 19:1-3 *Then Pilate took Jesus and scourged him. And the soldiers plaited a crown of thorns, and put it on his head, and arrayed him in a purple robe; they came up to him, saying, "Hail, King of the Jews!" and struck him with their hands.*

How can we tell if Jesus' past karma caused this? We can, however, see a graphic picture of meekness. The events of Golgotha must become real for us. We must enter into Jesus' experience as if it were happening to us. We must experience his meekness as the thorns stick into his scalp. We must experience his meekness when he is struck and mocked.

The more real this feeling of meekness is, the closer we are connected with our I AM. Steiner suggests that Jesus was joyful on the way to the cross. His joy would have come from his ability to connect with eternity, timelessness, which is what happens when we become conscious of our I AM. A true experience of meekness will ensure that we receive our inheritance.

Three: Disciplining our astral body

We cannot inherit the earth unless we discipline our astral (starry) body. Our astral nature is essentially concerned with motion and emotion. Plants do not have astral bodies and therefore can't move around like animals and humans. Our astral animates our body and gives us our elementary feelings. Also, it is through our astral that we are conscious beings. When our astral connection loosens at night during sleep we are not usually conscious. There are times during the night when our astral will connect up with our etheric body and we experience this as dreams.

The more we can control our astral body, the more refined are our actions and emotions. The more purified our astral, the more conscious we are. Because our astral body extends beyond our physical body, it is in touch with everything in our environment. The more aware we are of what is going on around us, the more spiritualised our astral.

Even though our astral is part of our spiritual nature, it is more attracted to our physical life than to our spiritual life. It is as if our astral wants to turn its back on its spiritual home and fully immerse itself in the pleasures of the physical world. In the Bible, the Greek word *sarx* (for flesh) is usually pointing to the astral body. In the prologue to the Gospel of St John we find some hints about our astral nature.

...to all who received him, who believed in his name, he gave power to become children of God; who were born, not of blood nor of the will of the flesh nor of the will of man, but of God. And the Word became flesh and dwelt among us, full of grace and truth; we have beheld his glory, glory as of the only Son from the Father. Jn 1:12-14

The will of the flesh, our astral's will, cannot give birth to the children of God. Only through connecting up with our I AM can we become children of God who are 'all who received' the I AM, who believed in the name I AM. Then Christ, the Logos, the Word, can dwell in our purified astral body. Reading verse 14 slightly differently gives us a clearer understanding of how the meek inherit the earth.

And the Word became flesh and dwelt within us, teaching us, as the radiance of the self-born Son of the Father, full of grace and truth. Jn 1:14

We are self-born when we connect up with our I AM through our own striving. Then we are set to receive the Father's inheritance.

It is the act of striving that prevents the astral from being distracted from its spiritual purpose. Furthermore, we can only purify it here, on earth, while it is connected to our physical body. This is a process of training, of using our will to direct our actions and feelings. Using our will in this way means that it becomes God's will.

There are many exercises described in esoteric literature which give our astral body a workout. We can say no to our habitual actions; eating and drinking to excess etc.. We can interrupt our daily routine and do something that we wouldn't normally do at a certain time of the day. Instead of reading the paper in the morning, we could do some gardening. We could put the car keys in a different place every day. Or we could put the kettle on the other side of the kitchen. This disrupts our automatic actions and stirs the forces in our whole being, awakening that which is dream-like within us. Then we will be meek, balanced, because we have taken possession of (inherited) our real earthly consciousness. In other words, we become conscious, no longer robotically habitual. It is our I AM that must indwell our physical body, not just our astral.

The most rigorous exercise to give our astral a work-out is to trace our steps backwards. Try taking the birds-eye-view from the ceiling and see yourself moving around your house. It is the view we get when we reverse a movie – try that on the video player to get a feel for it. We can speed it up or slow it down, and then practice it often in our imagination. It is particularly helpful at the end of the day before retiring to bed.

This astral purification strengthens us, and enlivens our soul, making us more aware. It also invigorates the Christ impulse within us, assisting us to calm our passions, desires and emotions. It isn't about rejecting desires; it is about feeling the desires and being conscious of keeping them in balance. When we do this, we release forces which enliven and energise our whole being.

Another powerful astral cleanser is when we take a sentence of esoteric truth and really work with it, thinking it through from all directions, striving to understand it more fully. We mustn't passively take in spiritual teachings without experiencing the discomfort of deep thought. By wrestling to comprehend spiritual truth, we purify our astral. It all depends on our inner participation, our meekness.

Four: *Anger must give birth to love*

In this third stage of becoming Christened, of changing our being into the very being of Christ, it is important for us to be able to still our astral body. In his Studies of the New Testament, Valentin Tomberg explains this very clearly. We must master the inner movements of our astral body so that it is our "I" that determines what takes place in our being.

The strongest impulse in our astral body is anger. The meek are those who are able to overcome anger when it is there and invoke it when there is no personal cause for it. Then we are managing the force of anger rather than it rising up within us independently.

Anger usually rises up when we want things to go differently; when our expectations are not met. This means that we are bucking against our karmic pattern. This karmic pattern has been carefully orchestrated to give us the greatest opportunity for spiritual growth. It is helpful to realise that the Luciferic beings encourage us to ignore karmic patterns because they want us to be free of the earth now. They are intent on being overly helpful by encouraging us to take shortcuts which will move us forward too quickly.

Anger is a misunderstood resource in our being. Anger management is a greatly misunderstood process. Suppressing anger, or expressing it in harmless ways, or even thinking differently to dissipate anger, actually hampers our spiritual development. Anger educates our soul by agitating it. When we experience the anger inwardly we are strengthened. The opposite occurs if we express the anger, for then we are weakened. By getting in touch with our anger we can regulate it and put it to good use.

Think about the feeling of anger. When we are angry we are consumed by the anger. Therefore, when we are angry we actually forget self. This passage to selflessness gives us a heightened awareness of our I AM. Through finely tuning our experience of anger, we can find that point where we resist expressing the anger outwardly and immediately, amazingly, we experience love. We mightn't recognise this at first, but through careful observation we will experience how love is born within us through anger. It is the same love that carried Jesus through the experience of Golgotha where he would have mastered his anger to enable him to express the purest love through the indwelling Christ.

If we are able to conquer our astral and its tendency to anger, the forces thereby freed assist our Imaginative consciousness. This then enables us to see the truth about the deed of Christ.

Being able to bring calm to our astral requires courage. In fact controlling and converting our anger actually creates this force we call courage. Then we are equipped to look at the naked truth – about self and about others. It is then important that we develop the presence of mind so that when our illusions are destroyed we don't lose faith in our fellow man no matter what they do. By overcoming anger, impatience, intolerance we develop the courage of faith which is necessary to endure truth.

Jesus then said to the Jews who had believed in him, "If you continue in my word, you are truly my disciples, and you will know the truth, and the truth will make you free." Jn 8:31-32

Truth, *aletheia*, means 'that reality lying at the basis of an appearance'. If we are strong enough, courageous enough, we are able to see beneath the surface to face truth. As soon as we achieve that we will experience freedom. Not freedom to do as we please, but an inner freedom to make choices – like using our anger. The outer world will not dictate how we feel, or how we act. Our thoughts will not be filled with the media's stereotypes. We also will repress the urge to impose our ideas on others. Our freedom automatically gives freedom to others because they are released from our expectations. This is the way of the meek. While we say that we need to develop these abilities so that we can inherit the earth, there are drawbacks as Jesus points out.

"If the world hates you, know that it has hated me before it hated you. If you were of the world, the world would love its own; but because you are not of the world, but I chose you out of the world, therefore the world hates you. Jn 15:18-19

Animosity is increasing everywhere in the world. This is a good thing because it gives us many opportunities to practice our anger management. Then we will have firsthand knowledge of the rich resource we have within us, one that is the necessary precursor to pure love, pure meekness and the ability to receive our inheritance.

Five: Higher and lower use of will

Central to contemplating the Beatitudes is the fact that they are also called the Sermon on the Mount. Whatever happens on a mountain indicates that it is revealed to higher consciousness. While these Beatitudes uncover spiritual standards by which we live our daily lives, they also point to the effects of our daily activities on the evolution of the world. This means that spiritual awakening is accompanied by cosmic responsibilities.

Those who study the esoteric teachings are well aware that these are crucial times. There are many forces hindering the breakthrough in consciousness that is due, if not overdue. We could say that we are in the midst of a battle of the wills. Not one strong will up against another strong will, but rather, how to use our will, if it is used at all!

Will can be seen like a cross in our being; inner and outer, upper and lower. Will is directly related to our body's activity - conscious or unconscious. Within us, the will is responsible for life-giving movements like digestion, the passage of fluids, etc.. Externally, it is through the directive forces of the will that we are able to move around in the world.

The higher and lower use of our will is directly related to how conscious we are and how we are connected to our I AM. If we manage to use our thinking to strengthen our will, as we must, we are then presented with the choice of expressing goodwill or misusing or misdirecting our will.

The meek are those who have great control of their will. They are not will-less, they actually have great strength of will. Their will is like a sword skilfully wielded. Their will is never misapplied, to self or to others. It is always used in the right measure.

At this point in evolution, as our spiritual consciousness is awakening, we must become much more conscious of what we create with our will forces. When we express our will it is often so that the other person will act differently. We want to influence others so that they meet our expectations. This is wilfulness and through it we create things in the astral worlds that will eventually come to pass. It is frightening to contemplate what we might have created in the astral worlds though our unconscious or semi-conscious wilfulness.

St. John gives us a picture of this possibility when he describes the actions of Simon Peter in the Garden of Gethsemane. He immediately contrasts it with the act of Divine will which comes to us in the image of the cup.

Then Simon Peter, having a sword, drew it and struck the high priest's slave and cut off his right ear. The slave's name was Malchus. Jesus said to Peter, "Put your sword into its sheath; shall I not drink the cup which the Father has given me?" Jn 18:10-11

The meek are those who have such a strong sense of self, such a strong connection with their I AM, that they don't need to always feel in control. If soldiers, our ideas of control, want to come poking about in our spiritual business, let them. They want to know exactly what is happening down to the last detail and they don't care how they find out. They can never let things unfold naturally. When the blindness of their actions meets the unthinking Peter, before you know it, off comes an ear.

Our sphere of the will can be found between the astral body and the "I". It is easy to see how it can pull one way or the other. If it pulls towards our body, it is unconscious, if it pulls towards our "I", it is conscious. It is a mighty force and it is the domain of the Ahrimanic spirits. These are the spirits of lies. We see it clearly at work again in Peter when he denied being a disciple of Jesus.

One of the servants of the high priest, a kinsman of the man whose ear Peter had cut off, asked, "Did I not see you in the garden with him?" Peter again denied it; and at once the cock crowed. Jn 18:26-27

When we work on our spiritual development, especially through meditation and other exercises, we awaken our will in our soul and spirit. This brings with it a deep responsibility. For this very reason spiritual teachings were kept secret in the past. It was well known that through the awakened will we can create things in the astral worlds that could arrest evolution. Now that the spiritual teachings are freely available, those who study them can, by example, reveal their true purpose in daily life – that is our sacred task.

The sword and the cup are the two symbols that reveal the work that we must do with our will forces so that we can inherit the earth. Our motto, given to us by St Paul, fosters our good will: Christ in us, the hope of glory. (Col 1:27)

4. BLESSED ARE THOSE WHO HUNGER AND THIRST FOR RIGHTEOUSNESS, FOR THEY WILL BE FILLED. MT 5:6

One: Ennobling our drives and desires

The beatification of our being happens when we allow our I AM to take control of every level of our body, soul and spirit. It is a process which only we can direct. It depends on the fertility of each of the members of our being; physical, etheric, astral, three soul levels and three spirit levels. We make these members fertile through striving to control the natural, automatic processes, habits and motives developed over our lifetime.

To assist us to accomplish this, simultaneously, we need to enhance the Christ power within us. This power is a seed to be tenderly nurtured. For the right outcome, these two processes must work co-operatively, otherwise an imbalance can occur; we can become overly individualistic or overly spiritual. To achieve the balance we need to be strongly motivated; our motives need to be as focussed as the drives of hunger and thirst. The story about the woman at the well can give us some clues about this Beatitude.

There came a woman of Samar'ia to draw water. Jesus said to her, "Give me a drink." For his disciples had gone away into the city to buy food. The Samaritan woman said to him, "How is it that you, a Jew, ask a drink of me, a woman of Samar'ia?" For Jews have no dealings with Samaritans. Jesus answered her, "If you knew the gift of God, and who it is that is saying to you, 'Give me a drink,' you would have asked him, and he would have given you living water." The woman said to him, "Sir, you have nothing to draw with, and the well is deep; where do you get that living water? Are you greater than our father Jacob, who gave us the well, and drank from it himself, and his sons, and his cattle?" Jesus said to her, "Every one who drinks of this water will thirst again, but whoever drinks of the water that I shall give him will never thirst; the water that I shall give him will become in him a spring of water welling up to eternal life." The woman said to him, "Sir, give me this water, that I may not thirst, nor come here to draw." Jn 4:7-15

First, we must thirst, then, when our I AM finds the fertile ground that it needs, and when we have nurtured the Christ Spirit within us, we will be filled with this living water. We will no longer depend on the physical world to satisfy us, we will experience the satisfaction that comes from rightly motivated spiritual development.

It is interesting that powerful drives like hunger and thirst should come up at this point. The fourth level of our being is found in our soul. If we acknowledge that the soul has three different expressions linked to feeling, thinking and willing, we can see that this fourth Beatitude relates to the first soul region associated with feeling. This sentient area of our soul is where the outside world enters into us. All that enters our soul is then processed in the second soul region where we think about the impressions, where we make sense of them and rationalise them.

It is in the first soul region that we ennoble the drives and desires that rise up from our body. In other words, here we control our astral urges to satisfy our hunger, thirst, passions etc. in an appropriate way. Here we also ennoble our motives. The woman of Samaria asked Jesus about his motives for asking her for a drink. When it comes to emotions and feelings we must always examine the motives behind everything we do. If our motives are not pure then the fertility of our being is affected. Any seedlings growing there will shrivel.

At this stage in evolution our lives are an initiation. What took place behind the closed doors of the mystery schools before the time of Christ now occurs in our daily lives. Modern initiation is about having a firsthand experience of our I AM. The procedure manual is found in the events of the life of Christ. Everything that he experienced, we will experience - within our consciousness. All the events and people represent the different areas of our consciousness that are affected by our I AM as it takes hold of each part of our being. How the I AM operates through our sentient soul differs to the way it operates through our etheric body and so on. Initially, for the etheric body, or the astral body, the "I" is an intruder.

The woman of Samaria treats Jesus like an intruder. *"How is it that you, a Jew, ask a drink of me, a woman of Samar'ia?"* The time of segregation has now been replaced by integration. All those who are connected with their I AM become part of a new community, a new fraternity that transcends beliefs and cultures. This is the bond of Christ. Wherever there is separation Christ is not to be found. Only through love and purity of motive can we find the living water.

Two: Harmony and balance

Righteousness is not part of our modern vocabulary. Righteousness is, however, uppermost in the mind of every human being in the world today. Righteousness, *dikaiosune*, means justice in terms of being just, balanced and in harmony. Justice is not about an 'eye for an eye' but rather it is a continual series of adjustments to restore balance and harmony.

We get the best sense of this word from the story of the three bears; the porridge was to be not too hot or too cold, but just right. Blessed are those who hunger and thirst for just-right-ness, for they will be filled. It is highly likely that this folk story was told to illustrate how we are each responsible for achieving balance in our own lives which in turn contributes to harmony in the culture of our community.

In the third century BC Aristotle wrote an entire book about *dikaiosune*. Aristotle's philosophy was a guide to living in a free society as equals rather than under the care of the tribal elder. This was a time when human consciousness went through a great upheaval. Direct experience of the spiritual world was diminishing to enable human beings to develop their ability to think. In these terms, Aristotle was actually the herald of the I AM because he was preparing humanity to become self-responsible, self-directed citizens. Through his insight into human nature he could see, however, that self-interest could sway human motives. He knew how important it was for us to be able to judge when things were 'just right'.

John speaks of the difficulty of getting things 'just right' in chapter 3. His use of the word evil in this passage points to not-right-ness. *And this is the judgment, that the light has come into the world, and men loved darkness rather than light, because their deeds were evil. For every one who does evil hates the light, and does not come to the light, lest his deeds should be exposed. But he who does what is true comes to the light, that it may be clearly seen that his deeds have been wrought in God.* Jn 3:19-21

The responsibility to get things right rests entirely with us. Read this passage again and replace the word 'light' with I AM. ... *the I AM has come into the world, and men loved [the] 'not-I AM' rather than the I AM, because their works were not right.*

So first, we must see that our works are not right. It takes enormous courage to face the fact that we are in the dark and many of our works – *erga* - are not right. This is why we must always be open to new ideas and new understandings. When faced with any situation in life, if we try to find twelve ways of looking at it, we will always be open to new possibilities. To do this we need to accept each one of the twelve ways as valid, (even if we don't fully agree with it). Then we will never be fixed on our own ideas. John tells us what this will mean for us: *He who is doing the truth - aletheia - comes to the I AM*. *Aletheia* means unhidden-ness, unconcealed. It means we un-hide the hidden facets of a situation to reach a full understanding of it.

John is also pointing out that there is a two-way action; our work and the I AM's work. We stay open by allowing the light to shine into all our works; and the I AM shines it's light into us, enlightening us.

Our works (our enterprises) are all about how we think, feel and act. These soul faculties are the I AM's instruments. We love the darkness when we let them operate habitually or unconsciously, or when we are lazy about looking for twelve different ways to look at things. Here we grope around, either lacking in confidence, or being over-confident, searching for what is 'just right'. We will only know what is right if we allow our I AM full use of its instruments.

In this process we must experience powerful cravings for the input of our I AM. Our perseverance depends on how hungry and thirsty we are. Light can be very blinding and we are often tempted to withdraw into the comfort of darkness. We must embrace the presence of Christ who will assist us to manage all these powerful influences in our body, soul and spirit that are driving us forward.

Jesus said to them, "I am the bread of life; he who comes to me shall not hunger, and he who believes in me shall never thirst. Jn 6:35

Our hunger cannot be satisfied and our thirst cannot be quenched until we first experience them. We must experience the 'too hot' and the 'too cold' to know what is 'just right'; then we will be filled. This filling is experienced when we have created the necessary harmony in our soul which is required for the presence of Christ to dwell there.

Three: Hunger and thirst for love

Hunger and thirst are essential life-processes. They ensure our survival in this physical world. They are an alarm telling us to fill up or face death.

This experience of hunger and thirst makes us inwardly aware of ourselves. We realise that we are self-enclosed beings; individual units separate from the outside world. This presents us with two choices; to feel alone and separated, or to extend ourselves to connect up with all that is external to us.

If our experience of separation overwhelms us we then draw things to ourselves in the hope of satisfying our hunger and thirst. Close scrutiny will reveal that we draw many things to ourselves from external sources because of our inner spiritual hunger and thirst. Whenever we look outside ourselves for satisfaction alarm bells should ring.

This is a warning that we are not hungering for just-right-ness. It means that we are satisfying our emptiness physically instead of spiritually. This can manifest in the simplest forms; in eating or drinking too much, shopping for things that we don't need, wanting others to demonstrate how they value us, and especially when we find it difficult to place ourselves in the other person's shoes, to name but a few.

Of course, the satisfaction from these physically satisfying things is fleeting. Our hunger and thirst can never be satisfied until we experience the sustenance that can only come from our I AM. Righteousness, *dikaiou sunesis* (understanding of the just) speaks intimately of the divine order of the universe. Each time we satisfy our hunger and thirst we should be mindful that the sole purpose of these feelings in our physical bodies is to point to the spiritual hunger and thirst that we must come to feel. In other words, they point us to Christ who left us with the penultimate and mysterious way to satisfy our hunger and thirst; the bread and the wine.

Jesus said to them, "I am the bread of life; he who comes to me shall not hunger, and he who believes in me shall never thirst. Jn 6:35

He also demonstrated, in one of the seven sayings from the cross, that thirst signifies that moment when the Christ spirit can fructify our I AM: *After this Jesus, knowing that all was now finished, said (to fulfil the scripture), "I thirst."* Jn 19:28 When we have this experience, then, "Not I, but Christ in me." becomes a reality for us.

Therefore, righteousness, dikaiosune (dik-ah-yos-oo'-nay) can only be found in our Christened I AM. Jesus said it; our I AM is the bread of life, without it we are empty. Until we are able to express ourselves from our I AM instead of our astral we will have cravings that cannot be satisfied. We will yearn for freedom but mostly experience the frustrating bondage of the physical world. We will also have to bear what we see as un-justness in the world.

Rev. Mario Schoenmaker spoke beautifully about the fourth Beatitude in 1989 at a retreat to mark St John's Tide. He said that the spiritualising of the sentient region of our soul works on our feeling and perception. "This enables [us] to feel the outpouring of human brotherly love, which is called righteousness. The word righteousness means 'to do right'. And to do right is to love is it not? That is then the universal principal of Christianity.

The person who hungers and thirsts for this all-ruling righteousness is the person who wants; not only do they feel that love deep down within self, but they want to share this with everyone. This is the person who hungers and thirsts for righteousness. What does the sentient soul feel in the physical body otherwise? Hunger - comes from the sentient soul? Thirst? Now we must learn to feel for spiritual things: to hunger and thirst after righteousness."

He goes on to say that the only lasting satisfaction we can possibly experience while we are in this physical body is the satisfaction that comes from our spiritual life. This satisfaction can only be ours when we actually experience the spiritual teachings, not just know them as theory. Furthermore, the spiritual teachings can only be a reality in our lives when we love each other with the purity and intensity that Christ loves us. *A new commandment I give to you, that you love one another; even as I have loved you, that you also love one another.* Jn 13:34 Then all division disappears; all opinions fall away and we are filled. After the filling, love pours from of us - that unmistakably Christened love.

Four: Difficulties arise when the I AM works in our consciousness

As we approach Advent we turn our attention to the birth of Christ, *the Holy and Righteous One*, as St. Paul calls him in Acts 3:14. Over the next four weeks we have the opportunity to prepare for the birth of Christ in our consciousness. If we attune ourselves, we can become conscious of the angels drawing near to assist with, and witness, this birth.

The main message of the fourth Beatitude is that we need to crave the presence of Christ in our being. Do we crave his presence as much as we crave food or water? When we have translated the physical power of hungering and thirsting into the real spiritual task that it is, then we must experience the just-right balance of our soul forces; feeling, thinking and willing. For our feelings to be balanced we always need the right amount of support from our thinking and our will. When thinking comes to the fore, the just-right amount of feeling and will should be working in the background. If these soul forces work unsupported then our thinking is wonky, or our feelings will be too hot or too cold, or wilfulness dominates.

At this present time in the evolution of our consciousness we are particularly working with the will forces in our being. Mastery of our will is a prerequisite to achieving a state of righteousness. The will is associated with the Father and the Father forces are not at work in us until we have permeated our will with Christ. This may shed some light on why the Father is a mysterious concept. He is always hidden from view. It is like when a child is created; the work of the mother is very visible as her stomach grows, but the work of the father's sperm remains invisible.

Jesus speaks a lot about the Father in his farewell discourses in John Chapters 14-17. He even connects the Father to righteousness ....

Nevertheless I tell you the truth: it is to your advantage that I go away, for if I do not go away, the Counselor [Holy Spirit] will not come to you; but if I go, I will send him to you. And when he comes, he will convince the world concerning sin and righteousness and judgment: concerning sin, because they do not believe in me; concerning righteousness, because I go to the Father, and you will see me no more; concerning judgment, because the ruler of this world is judged. Jn16:7-11

This passage is a guide for our spiritual development. It points directly to our need to claim our I AM which is removed from us, so that through our own volition, we prepare our being as a suitable instrument. *"A little while, and you will see me no more; again a little while, and you will see me."* Jn 16:16… a few verses later John talks about the anguish of birth being replaced by the joy of the child. This will be our experience as our I AM takes up its rightful place in our consciousness.

Our task is to prepare ourselves so that our I AM can live in us like a driving force, continually bringing to birth a higher consciousness. Now, through our own initiative, we must navigate the conditions of life – sin, righteousness and judgment. Jesus tells us that it happens in a certain order.

First, we work with the Holy Spirit who assists us to stop sinning. Sin, *hamartia*, means to miss the mark. In our spiritual development we need to be on target more of the time. We miss the mark when we don't think beyond the materialistic view of life. The Holy Spirit, the Spirit of truth, assists us to see behind outer appearances to the etheric presence of Christ woven in and around this earth.

Then, we have a new relationship with Christ - *you will see me no more* is better translated, "you no longer behold me". We no longer behold Christ (outside us) because we experience him within us. Then we become the Righteous One as Christ and the Father become one in our being.

Finally, the matter of judgment, *krisis*, when *the ruler of this earth is judged*. The rulers of this earth are the ones who obscure our spiritual vision. It is when we see their motives and deeds that they are automatically judged. This judging occurs through life's many crises. What happens when we have to deal with crisis? We have to adjust ourselves; we have to restore balance in our lives. The scales are the great symbol of judgment; we place a weight on one side or the other to restore the right balance. When crises happen in our lives it indicates that our I AM is gaining some independent expression in our being. Our spiritual vision automatically judges whatever has been obstructing us. Then we know that we are blessed and filled.

5. BLESSED ARE THE MERCIFUL, FOR THEY WILL BE SHOWN MERCY. MT 5:7

One: Love one another

The fifth Beatitude reveals to us what must take place in the second region of our soul where we use our intellect. This is the place of reason within us; this is where we decide what to think and what not to think. If our will supports our thinking adequately, our thoughts will be rigorous; if not, they will be lazy. With the right support, we will readily think new thoughts, rather than habitual ones.

In our journey to become Christened, blessed, our thoughts must become more and more merciful. Merciful, *eleēmones*, means that we actively experience the other person as if we were them. So we think about others as we would like them to think about us. Since it is our instinct to think of ourselves first, when we are truly merciful we think of others just as much as we think of ourselves. Note: not more than ourselves, for that is to be altruistic.

In our second soul region we make sense of all that streams into us through our first soul region. In our mind-soul (second region) we assess the value of all that enters into our consciousness. Sometimes we don't fully value a thing because of one bad experience. Through mercy we can re-value and reassess our attitude to life. Therefore mercy is directly linked to the activity of judging. The quality of our judging depends on the health of our first soul region, our sentient soul.

In the presence of mercy, our judging will not only be based on the past and the present, but will also take into account the future. We move from being just to being kind. When we are able to look through the eyes of our I AM we can understand why some people act the way they do. Then our judging takes on a new tone.

Valentin Tomberg, in his New Testament Studies, gives a beautiful metaphor about our intellect. He says that our judging will be as sharp and clear as sunlight, but also as warm. Our thinking will soften, not to become vague, but to become merciful.

If we observe our thinking carefully, we will notice that many of our thoughts are cold, harsh and judgemental. We wouldn't dream of saying some of the things that we think. These are the very thoughts that must become merciful. When the content of our thinking becomes sharp - more conscious - but also soft and warm, this means that we are experiencing the presence of Christ in our souls.

Mercy can mean compassion, kindness, sympathy and so on, but it can be summed up in these words of Jesus:

These things I have spoken to you, that my joy may be in you, and that your joy may be full. "This is my commandment, that you love one another as I have loved you. Greater love has no man than this, that a man lay down his life for his friends. You are my friends if you do what I command you. Jn 15:11-14

Imagine! What would it be like to have the joy of Christ in us? *Chara* is the Greek word for joy and it is very similar to grace, *charis*. Both these words have a connection to the expression of mercy.

When it comes to laying down one's life, *psuche*, for our friends – *psuche* means soul – it indicates that our souls naturally think of the greater good. Instead of always thinking about what will be good for us, increasingly we must think in terms of what is best for all of us. If that means we give a little, become a little less self-centred, then we will be blessed and shown mercy.

We could say that mercy is the next step after righteousness;

where justice becomes forgiveness. At its foundation it is love, *agape*. To the extent that we can love others is the extent to which we will be shown mercy. However, we should realise that what seems merciless to us may, in fact, be great mercy in the long run.

Paul, in his Epistle to Titus sheds even more light on the nature of mercy.

... but when the goodness and loving kindness of God our Savior appeared, he saved us, not because of deeds done by us in righteousness, but in virtue of his own mercy, by the washing of regeneration and renewal in the Holy Spirit, which he poured out upon us richly through Jesus Christ our Savior, so that we might be justified by his grace and become heirs in hope of eternal life. Titus 3:5-7

Eternal life, of course, is when we live life through our I AM and allow Christ to reign in our beings – and this can happen now.

Two: Goodwill

The Sermon on the Mount is described in Matthew's Gospel and the disciple Matthew represents the will faculty within us. That mysterious force which, out of necessity, keeps our body alive but which also gives us the possibility of freedom.

The enigma of necessity and freedom is one of the greatest mysteries of the human being. The fulcrum for necessity and freedom is love. John is all about love which makes his Gospel a good place to look for further advice about living these Beatitudes daily in our lives.

Since the fifth Beatitude focuses on the soul faculty of thinking then our quest is about how to use our thinking in a balanced way? How often are our thoughts supported by our will and balanced by love? When they are, we express goodwill.

Think about that other 'sermon on the mount', the Ten Commandments. The gods withdrew, they let go our hand and told us to get on with life without their direction. Because we were not used to making decisions for ourselves a few guidelines were put in place. All our feelings, thoughts and actions were now to be governed by the fear of 'Thou shalt not', a law imposed on us externally.

When Jesus came he changed things again. His Sermon on the Mount, expressed in these Beatitudes, while built on the foundation of the Commandments, now said that, in freedom, humanity can act out of their own I AM. Again, we needed some guidelines but now, from within, it is up to us to interpret them and live by them. Unless we do, we cannot become Christened, blessed.

This fifth Beatitude tells us that if we want to become Christened we have to be merciful, and we do indeed. When we think about being merciful isn't our first thought about being merciful towards others? We contemplate how we can change the way we think about others, judge others. We consider how can we be more compassionate to others? But how merciful are we to ourselves?

When someone tells us that we have done something wrong, hurt their feelings or upset them in some way, how much agony do we experience? When they tell us that they don't agree with us, or don't like us, how much pain do we feel? The solution is not to become blazé about criticism but to accept it as a fact and to be merciful to ourselves about it. To do this we must contain our reaction and in that moment a sense of compassion for ourselves is released within us. We reach a new acceptance of who we are because the spiritual force released from our containment makes us aware of whom we will become. In such moments we experience our I AM, our True Self, our full potential, and we know that we want to experience it more and more.

Once we begin to master being merciful to ourselves we will increasingly be merciful to others. We will be more embracing of others. We will value them more even if we do not like them and the things that they do. We won't be sucked into the automatic soul reaction of like or dislike. This new appreciation for others will arise because as we have seen our own potential, we now see their potential. This is mercy. This is the I AM taking control of our thinking.

When our I AM has regular access to our soul we see things in a much better perspective. We see the good and the bad in everything without gravitating to one or the other with our thinking and our judging. We fully appreciate that there can be no shadows without the light. Through our I AM we can see the purpose of the darkest shadow, and we can bear the brightest light. In our observation we become the interested observer. John puts it well in the following verses;

Now when he was in Jerusalem at the Passover feast, many believed in his name when they saw the signs which he did; but Jesus did not trust himself to them, because he knew [from above] all men and needed no one to bear witness of man; for he himself knew what was in man. John 2:23-25

Don't be mesmerised by signs and wonders, they won't reveal to you the truth about the human being. The truth about the human being can only be found in the I AM - from above. No-one outside us can 'bear witness' to the truth of our being, our true self. We must experience it firsthand. When we do, signs will not impress us because they pale into insignificance compared with experiencing our I AM. Then we will be merciful and receive mercy.

Three: Through love we give birth to our I AM

In the previous two reflections we looked at being merciful to others as well as being merciful to ourselves. Let us now consider how we receive mercy. Is it simply a catch-cry, "Lord, have mercy on me"? Isn't that relying on something outside ourselves over which we have no control? It might happen, but then again it might not.

Furthermore, who do we mean when we say 'Lord'? Are we attempting to invoke the benevolence of God? Very often, when the word 'Lord' is used it actually means our I AM. In the Bible, from the outset of his ministry, Jesus is referred to as Lord Jesus. Jesus says, in John 13:13, *"You call me Teacher and Lord; and you are right, for so **I am**."*

So we are invoking our I AM which is outside us and has a (mostly) tenuous connection to us. However, we don't need to sit back and ask to receive mercy. We actually attract mercy when we develop a merciful attitude within us. Then we will be shown mercy – from the Lord, from our I AM. This mercy is simply a state of being that we can experience when we are in tune with our Higher Self. As we become more and more merciful we develop a spiritual force within us that is like a magnet – an I AM magnet!

It is not a matter of wondering if we will be shown mercy or not for there is nothing uncertain about our I AM. It is our eternal being, we can be absolutely certain that it is present in our lives, and it has a plan. We can co-operate with this plan or we can allow our astral to thwart the plan. The only possible way to be shown mercy is to co-operate with our I AM.

We do need to realise that the I AM is not about feel-good moments. Feel-good moments are very frequently not benevolent. Our I AM is about being conscious and to be conscious can be quite uncomfortable – especially when we experience things that we do not like, things that make us uncomfortable. The reason for the discomfort is because our astral is being disturbed. Our astral body is the seat of pain; if we have transformed our astral then we can bear the pain. Look at all the instances in the Bible when pain was inflicted on Jesus. The I AM can bear this pain because it's eye is on the prize.

In fact, we have at our disposal the most potent analgesic; we don't need a prescription, it is freely available. It is called love, *agape*.

A new commandment I give to you, that you love one another; even as I have loved you, that you also love one another. By this all men will know that you are my disciples, if you have love for one another." Jn 13:34-35

Christmas provides us with the spiritual opportunity to give birth to this love. The Father conceived this love and Jesus, the I AM, brings it into the physical. It gestates in our soul until it reaches full term and our soul goes into labour. John includes this story of mercy in his Gospel in Ch 15.

As the Father has loved me, so have I loved you; abide in my love. If you keep my commandments, you will abide in my love, just as I have kept my Father's commandments and abide in his love. Jn 15:9-10

The Christmas images tell the story. In the baby Jesus we see the gift of nature that forms his physical vehicle. We also see the spiritual purity of Mary, our soul, who is able to give birth. Then, when conditions are right, Jesus, the I AM, can enter. What are the right conditions? The right conditions only exist when we are conscious. When we can use our intellect, our thinking, and say, "I love." This is not love that flows to others because we like them, or because they agree with us, or because they give us something we want. This is love that we experience for people that we perhaps do not like, who perhaps refuse to agree with us or give us what we want. This is love that wells up in us when we truly experience compassion for others. This is agape, the very substance of the I AM, that creates unity.

As we travel through these last few days towards Christmas we can try to become a little more conscious. We can mentally generate more love for some of the people around us, especially the ones who annoy us. We can have compassion for them as they, too, labour to give birth to their I AM in their soul.

Then, we can follow the maturation process through the year ahead; from birth to baptism to the cross, to resurrection. The more conscious we are, the more we experience *agape*, Christ will fill our I AM and we will be radiant life-filled lights in the cosmos.

Four: Compassion: the balance between mercy and judgment

When we view our nine-fold being as physical, etheric and astral - our physical vehicles in this world, then our three levels of soul – called Sentient Soul, Mind Soul, and Consciousness Soul, in that order - and three levels of spirit – Imagination, Inspiration and Intuition, we can see that the Intellectual or Mind soul, which this Beatitude speaks of, is the actual centre of our being. This would be one of the reasons that our I AM is anchored here and first becomes active here. This is where we are self-thinking beings. This is where the Word can speak within us. *In the beginning was the Word, and the Word was with God, and the Word was [a] God.* Jn 1:1

Furthermore, at the time of Jesus Christ we were developing this area of our soul, as we are developing our Consciousness or Spiritual Soul now. When we developed our Mind Soul we learned to think for ourselves and closed off our psychic (mindless) tendencies.

In tune with this central core of our being it is significant that the fifth Beatitude tells us that unless, out of our own volition, we are merciful we will not be shown mercy. Now it is no longer an "eye for and eye and a tooth for a tooth"; now we must use our reasoning capacities to respond in a more reasonable way. The more we can do this, the more merciful we will be. We could equally say that unless we are compassionate, we will not be shown compassion. Unless we are kind, we will not be shown kindness. Or unless we love, we will not be loved. Unless we give, we will not receive.

This Beatitude stresses the self-reliance of the human being. It is up to us to be merciful; no-one can do it for us. Out of our own volition we must find what it is to be merciful. Not even God will give us this mercy unless we first discover how to express. Nor does this mercy need to be physically expressed; our thinking is the place where mercy starts. Whenever we begin to think damaging and critical thoughts about others we must quickly arrest them.

Also, this fifth Beatitude speaks beautifully of the balance, the harmony, that must exist in our mind; breathing out to be able to breathe in. This is how our mind must work; always the tidal ebb and flow, never stagnant. Our ideas must breathe otherwise, like stale air in our lungs, suffocation will result.

Our ideas must also be alive to the spiritual worlds, not just duplicates of someone else's ideas. When our ideas are in tune with the ever-evolving cosmos we echo the words of St John's prologue: *And the Word became flesh and dwelt among us, full of grace and truth; we have beheld his glory, glory as of the only* (the self-born) *Son from the Father.* Jn 1:14

This glory shines from those who have merciful thoughts, thoughts that are full of grace and truth. It is the glory of those who are self-born. They give birth to their I AM out of their own volition, not the Father's.

Then John reminds us: *For the law was given through Moses; grace and truth came through Jesus Christ.* Jn 1:17

Our task is to become more aware of our thinking and to guide it towards the side of mercy. Not to gloss over things in a genial, positive-thinking sort of way but to always strive for the grace-and-truth way. There are many ways to do this and many more will be discovered through our own individual work in this area. One thing we can do, for instance, is that in adversity we can give prominence to the advantages instead of the disadvantages.

When it comes to our thinking we must always be mindful of the need to breathe out as much as we breathe in. It is entirely up to us to create this balance in our mind. Only in this balance can be become merciful, compassionate. Compassion is found in the right balance of mercy and judgment. We must find the harmony; not too lenient, not too severe, not too soft, not too harsh. Our judging becomes discernment and our mercy becomes wise kindness when we are at our most compassionate.

When we make room for our I AM in our soul, then, blessed, Christened, we can be. To be Christened is to be like Jesus Christ, the great high priest. When we are able to express ourselves through our I AM, our priestly nature can be revealed, not before. The Letter to the Hebrews speaks of Jesus, the I AM, becoming merciful: *Therefore he had to be made like his brethren in every respect* (making the same journey of spiritual development), *so that he might become a merciful and faithful high* [true] *priest in the service of God...* Hb 2:17 That, too, is our goal.

6. BLESSED ARE THE PURE IN HEART, FOR THEY WILL SEE GOD. MT 5:8

One: Good-will, pure motives

The sixth Beatitude will assist us to understand how we become blessed when the Christ Impulse enters into the uppermost region of our soul; our consciousness or spiritual soul. In the evolution of consciousness this is the area of our soul that we are developing at present.

When our I AM is able to work into these soul forces in concert with the awakened presence of Christ, then our will becomes goodwill. Our intentions are formed out of the right motives. Our conscience and moral ethics flow from the Christ within. These are the cathartic experiences in our lives. We always feel a deep purity in our heart at these times.

The Greek word for pure is *katharos* which means clean, free of impurities, uncontaminated. Because the heart is the centre of our blood circulation this Beatitude points to the need for our blood to be cleansed, purified. Our blood is the physical expression of our I AM, it is the fire within us. If our blood is not pure then the I AM has difficulty connecting with our consciousness.

We must never forget that this material world works against our becoming conscious of our true self, our I AM. The world wants us to believe that our ego, the reflection of the I AM, is our real self.

This is like saying that the reflection that we see in the mirror is really us. These ideas need purifying, cleansing of error.

In John 13, when Jesus washes the feet of the disciples at the Last Supper he indicates the importance of being clean. *Jesus said to him, "He who has bathed does not need to wash, except for his feet, but he is clean all over; and you are clean, but not every one of you." For he knew who was to betray him; that was why he said, "You are not all clean."* John 13:10-11

This cleanliness, this purity is to do with the different forces in our being. Judas betrayed Jesus because he allowed Satan, Ahriman to control his consciousness. We can say that this was necessary, and perhaps it was, but was Judas conscious of it? Could he have been conscious of it? These questions remain.

The opposing forces do have their place in evolution; however, they do not always stay in their allotted place. Whenever we are unconscious these forces have the opportunity to work outside their allocated sphere of influence. This is how we become unclean. They confuse our thinking and muddle our motives.

In the text it seems strange that Jesus says; *"He who has bathed does not need to wash, except for his feet, but he is clean all over"* This is surely a reference to the pure heart. Jesus is possibly referring to the ritual bathing of the time which, as an outward ceremony, can do nothing unless our inner motives are pure. Since the time of Christ we have taken responsibility for our own purification. The problem is that we can't know what is pure unless we are strongly connected to our I AM and the presence of Christ irradiates our consciousness.

There is a wonderful meditation described in Tau Malachi's book, The Gnosis of the Cosmic Christ. We are encouraged to experience our heart pulsating within and behind with the radiant light of Christ. Then, we breathe in our difficulties and allow them to dissolve in this light. Then we breathe out light in its place.

The interesting thing here is that so often these meditations encourage us to breathe out our difficulties. In his Fifth Gospel, Rudolf Steiner talks about the consequences of this in relation to the Essene's purifying rituals. He describes Jesus seeing the two figures of Ahriman and Lucifer at the gate of the Essene compound, forbidden to enter, then, how they "made their way all the more into other human beings."

These are the ways of those who place themselves first. As long as we are ok, let the other person take care of themselves. This is not the way of the I AM. The I AM assists us to be conscious of the consequences of our actions. We are able to have the other person's experience as if it were our own. In the purity of our heart the anti-forces cannot use our unconscious minds. Here lies the secret of thinking with the heart and loving with the mind. The active presence of Christ, working with our I AM, loves. It never seeks to gain advantage over others, it just loves. Furthermore, there is an innocence about this love which is alien to the clever, modern mind. Such are the pure in heart and, of course, they will see God.

Two: The spiritual nature of our heart

Our heart occupies a place of honour in our being. It connects us to what lies deep within us. We innately know that our heart also connects us to our spiritual identity, our true being, our I AM.

Yet clever, modern minds mostly describe it as a mechanical pump. The ticker which we hope will continue to tick so that we can have a long physical life. While our physical life is, of course, very important, this Beatitude speaks of our spiritual and soul life.

When we are surrounded by worldly ideas it takes quite a lot of effort to remind ourselves that we are more than a physical body. As spiritual beings we attach ourselves to a physical vehicle so that we can spend some time on this earth to further develop our consciousness. Of our own volition we must become conscious enough to see God. While we can't see God, we are not conscious and our hearts are not pure.

Jesus could see God. He is our example. *No one has ever seen God; the only Son, who is in the bosom of the Father, he has made him known.* Jn 1:18

So how do we purify our heart? A good place to start is to understand the exact nature of our heart.

Firstly, we must discover that our heart is not a pump. We can't do this effectively by simply accepting what others say; we must experience the reality of it. The best place to begin is to have a real experience of how our body is controlled by our soul. Whatever happens in our body is directed by our soul. If we are to quench our thirst, for example, a signal from our body enters our soul and in our soul we work out how to get a drink. We decide which drink would best satisfy our thirst. We go through the selection of all the drinks that are available to us and we choose the one that appeals most. This is the work of our soul as it feels, thinks and wills and, in turn, affects our body.

There are other ways to experience the work of our soul. When we experience fear, the fear arises in our soul. Automatically we turn pale because the blood flow to the surface of our skin is interrupted. Our blood is busy pulsing deep within us and triggering physical responses to our soul's experience. It is the soul that affects our adrenalin; the flow of adrenalin doesn't happen all by itself. On the other hand, when we feel shame, the blood flow to the skin is increased and we blush.

If we observe our own experience of fear and shame in our soul we can more easily accept that the mobility of our blood is directed by our soul. Steiner's words then make more sense when he says: "The movements of the heart are not the cause, but the consequence of the pulsation of the blood." [Cosmic Memory Ch 18]

There are other experiences that we connect to our heart, and therefore our soul, for instance, joy and sorrow. We also say that we are soft hearted or hard hearted. Jesus says *"Do not let your hearts be troubled. Believe in God, believe also in me."* Jn 14:1

Our hearts are very troubled as we try to make sense of this world. How can we make sense of the violence; the rise of murderous teenagers, of suicide, of drug and alcohol abuse, of hopelessness, soullessness? Then, at the mention of God, comes anger. How could there be a God in the face of life's events!

When Jesus says *"believe also in me"* he is telling us to believe in our I AM. God is not to blame for anything, the responsibility sits with us. Our primary responsibility is to believe in our I AM. To believe is to trust that we have an I AM and that it is trying to direct our lives. Again, we have to work on imagining how this happens. Our I AM is like the conductor of the orchestra. This conductor is trying to direct our feeling, thinking and will so that certain harmonies and disharmonies occur in our soul and body which will ultimately make us more conscious.

Trouble is, while we are not aware of the conductor, our hearts are troubled. We act in habitual ways and our thoughts exclude the spiritual reality of our being and our purpose.

If we can just put some more effort into creating images of how our soul and I AM interact with our body, our thinking will become alive with new understandings. This will affect the way our blood flows which will affect the beat of our heart. When the rhythm of our heart beats in time with our I AM we love. The pure-hearted see God because they love.

Three: Conscience

This Beatitude speaks to us about our developing consciousness soul. At this point in evolution we must learn to use this part of our soul consciously, whereas in the past it operated instinctively. As we become more aware of how this area of our soul works, as we learn to push the buttons, so to speak, we become more conscious of our place in the world as physical human beings. It is only through our physical body that we become self-conscious beings. We become more and more aware of our separation from our environment and from other people. This is where true individuality begins.

The problem is that when we become more aware of our physical existence we forfeit our awareness of our spiritual existence. We could say that this area of our soul is our heightened awareness. Through it we learn how to maintain the delicate balance between leaning too much towards the physical or to the spiritual.

Yet all around us we see that the physical body is over-emphasised. Everywhere our attention is directed to our bodies. Are we eating too much or too little, do we need surgery to change how we look? Are we wearing the right fashion, should we take up another fanatical exercise or eating regime, and so on? In these ways the physical is elevated, physically instead of spiritually.

We mustn't forget that our physical body is simply the vehicle for our soul and spirit; through it we can develop our independence and deflect the guidance of spiritual beings. We must also remember that it is a process; consciousness-soul training-wheels are necessary. We know from experience that we will fall off the bike a few times before we learn to ride it properly.

This phase in our development often means that we have to experience life more fully as far as bodies are concerned; although not by being too self-indulgent or too aesthetic.

Another sign of the development of this area of our soul is our consuming self-interest. Even with the best intentions, it is excruciatingly difficult for us to see how even our smallest actions impact on others.

Through this picture of adversity we should be alert to the

benefits, which is human conscience in embryo. We are getting better and better at knowing what is good and what is bad - spiritually.

The pure hearted are those who have developed a finely tuned conscience. From within they are able to keep the balance between what is good and what it bad. They are not goody-goodies and they are not badies; they are aware of both sides and know how to maintain the equilibrium. So how do we develop our conscience?

Our conscience is developed when, as children, we learn right from wrong. We learn this, not from being taught, but by the example of our family and our teachers. Our conscience is further developed when our connection with our I AM is strengthened. In fact, if we didn't have the right examples of honesty, fairness and ethics in our childhood, expressing ourselves through our I AM overrides this.

Furthermore, conscience is all about how we use our will. Only though the possibility of error or impurity does our free will develop. It is not about saying a thing is right or wrong, it is about using our inner force to achieve a balance between the two. If there were only two ways; good and evil, then we could quite easily be able to choose to do the good and avoid the bad. This is unbalanced and does not allow us to develop our god-given ability make choices.

It is clear that conscience is at the heart of the problems of our modern culture. We are assailed from all sides by the actions of others, but also their thoughts. If we see human thoughts as forces then it doesn't take much to imagine the kinds of forces weaving in and around us. With a pure heart, however, we can look on our current situation with hope. The kind of hope that moves these forces in a forward direction to a time when more and more people will express themselves through their I AM. Then conscience will operate automatically. We will naturally act towards others as we would like them to act towards us.

External laws, then, will be obsolete for we will operate under the new commandment: *A new commandment I give to you, that you love one another; even as I have loved you, that you also love one another.* Jn 13:34.

Four: Perceiving Christ

The pure in heart are those whose conscience is pure. We don't have to work hard to have a pure conscience. We just have to see Christ and our conscience is immediately pure. If we can see Christ then we also see God as Jesus tells us several times in John's Gospel. So how do we see Christ? The disciple Philip had a problem with this.

Jesus said to him, "Have I been with you so long, and yet you do not know me, Philip? He who has seen me has seen the Father; how can you say, 'Show us the Father'? Jn 14:9

The Greek word 'seen' that John chose to use is from the word *Horao*. In the Beatitude, St. Matthew uses the word *Optanomai*. Both these words for 'see' are related to inner perceiving. We see and know; it is like perceiving with our eyes as well our mind. We see esoterically, beneath the surface of things.

We are actually more perceptive than we realise. Our education obscures our inner perceptiveness; it has been conditioned out of us. For instance, when we study spiritual principles our modern minds often want to separate things into components - which is fine while we are developing our understanding – but then we can forget to 'see' the complete picture. It is as if we need two sets of eyes; one for seeing the physical and one for seeing the spiritual. This is not the case however, all we need is to be born anew.

*"Truly, truly, I say to you, unless one is born anew, he cannot **see** the kingdom of God." Jn 3:3*

With this reborn perception we are enabled to see the complete picture, the whole kingdom. Then we will see who we really are. What we know of ourselves is only half the story. This new birth is a resurrection of consciousness through which we can see our I AM, Christ, the Father, the Holy Spirit and all the other spiritual beings responsible for upholding the earth and us – the kingdom of God.

Through this kind of seeing we develop our awareness of the Christ Impulse in us and around us – which is, of course, also the kingdom of God. Jesus may well ask us this question, *"Have I been with you so long, and yet you do not know me?*

Jesus, who represents our I AM, wants us to realise that if we can know our true selves, our I AM, then we will see the spiritual reality the surrounds us.

What isn't always so clear to us is that the power and presence of the Christ actually depends on us. The Trinity, with the assistance of the beings of the spiritual hierarchy, facilitated the entry of Christ into the body of Jesus. Now, we must facilitate the presence of this Impulse so that it can make itself known, perceived, on this earth. Every time we have a genuine experience of the Christ Impulse we add to it, we enlarge it and increase its power.

For this we need a pure heart. Our spiritual experiences, our moments of ecstasy can sometimes be the work of Lucifer. He wants to take us away from the earth, relieve us from the heaviness and difficulties of the earth. Ahriman pulls us the other way. He wants us to feel powerful and knowledgeable by enlarging our intellectual thoughts. The Christ Impulse is the fulcrum.

Through the Christ Impulse we can be the interested observer, not too connected with life's events, not too distant. Ready to take responsibility for our actions and our karma but not consumed by them. We are able to place ourselves into the souls of others so that they feel our companionship and our compassion; but not intrusively. We don't judge but rather observe with interest the choices people make. In other words, we see through the eyes of Christ.

Through the Christ Impulse we are able to take in the full panorama while maintaining equilibrium. We see and know all sides of things, we recognise the good and the not so good and we stand in the middle developing our pure heart. We echo John's powerful words when he says, "Our I AM is *the way, and the truth, and the life; no one comes to the Father, but by* the I AM. *If you had known the* I AM, *you would have known my Father also; henceforth you know him and have seen him.*" Jn 14:6-7

The hard part for us is to accepting that we already see God. We just have to become aware of this seeing. Horao means that we have to shake off our education and remind ourselves of Paul's words: *I can do* (SEE) *all things in him who strengthens me.* Php 4:13

Five: Christ the purifier

Pure, *katharos*, is about being cleansed. This is not something that we do once but something that we must do continually. The only substance that can cleanse us is the Christ Impulse. The impurities to be cleansed are all the activities within us that stem from the opposing forces.

In St. John's Gospel there is a powerful image of the variety of forces that go about their business within us when we forget to make ourselves *the temple of the living God.* 2 Co 6:16

St John describes the scene graphically. *In the temple he found those who were selling oxen and sheep and pigeons, and the money-changers at their business. And making a whip of cords, he drove them all, with the sheep and oxen, out of the temple; and he poured out the coins of the money-changers and overturned their tables. And he told those who sold the pigeons, "Take these things away; you shall not make my Father's house a house of trade."* Jn 2:14-16

When all this trade takes place in our being there is no room for the living God. To be pure in heart and to see God we need to get a rush from our inner experience of the Christ Impulse. This rush, or quickening is like a whip of cords which drives out all those forces that have set up their market within us.

At the market are buyers and sellers, on opposite sides of the table. This creates division because each one wants the advantage. Buyers and sellers are the power brokers and we find them everywhere in our modern world. Especially in economics and trade which have become today's God. Money represents energy and today it is manipulated to the nth degree. The world's soul is almost extinguished by the lack of principles in modern commerce.

What happens to the souls of people when multimillion dollar companies insist that employees report for work when there is no work to do, simply to avoid paying their redundancy packages? If the Christ Impulse purified the hearts of the management of these companies they could never make such decisions. When the Christ Impulse is obscured in this way the soul of world is damaged.

The only purity that is available to us is found in the Christ Impulse; those pure forces that were brought to earth through the mystery of Golgotha. We can only be pure in heart by cleansing our temples of the energy traders who replace our purity with a superficial, materialistic consciousness.

This purity arises when we do simple things like withholding judgements, being courageous, being humble, experiencing real compassion, gratitude and grace, just to name a few. And not just when it is easy to do so, but even when we are we are in the grip of a karmic opportunity.

It is in these ways that we remind ourselves that Christ incarnated to purify our physical body, our temple. Unless it is purified of all the contaminating forces we cannot be the temple of the living God, the Christened I AM.

Furthermore, as we awaken the Christ Impulse within us we increase the power of the Christ Impulse in the world. Then we become co-workers with Christ. In fact, we actually become Christ and we do the work that he does, and some. John tells us how this works;

"Truly, truly, I say to you, he who believes in me will also do the works that I do; and greater works than these will he do, because I go to the Father. Whatever you ask in my name, I will do it, that the Father may be glorified in the Son; if you ask anything in my name, I will do it. Jn 14:12-14

It is very humbling indeed to realise that the Christ Impulse depends on us. It is even more humbling to realise and accept that we are gods; *Jesus answered them, "Is it not written in your law, 'I said, you are gods'? If he called them gods to whom the word of God came (and scripture cannot be broken), do you say of him whom the Father consecrated and sent into the world, 'You are blaspheming,' because I said, 'I am the Son of God'?* Jn 10:34-36

This actually means our purified hearts can assist others to purify their hearts. Those who do this work are the pioneers opening the way for others, making it easier for them. With a pure heart we then see, recognise, the god that they are becoming.

7. BLESSED ARE THE PEACEMAKERS, FOR THEY WILL BE CALLED SONS OF GOD. MT 5:9

One: Balance, within and without

The first five Beatitudes speak to us about our inner personal development. They give us ways of understanding our developing consciousness as it applies to ourselves and our inner soul levels. The sixth Beatitude, "Blessed are the pure in heart for they shall see God." begins to direct our attention beyond ourselves. Even though it still deals with the development of our inner soul levels, here we reach our peak soul experience. As we learn to use the third soul region, the one that is closest to our spirit, automatically our spiritual consciousness becomes engaged. It is here that we start to become aware of how all the levels of our being flow into each other to create harmony – or not.

So the seventh Beatitude heralds the beginning of our understanding, and even experience, of the three levels of our spiritual consciousness. These begin to become active as our I AM connects with those aspects of our being that make physical life possible; our astral, etheric and physical bodies. This doesn't necessarily happen in any order, and it won't happen fully for many, many lifetimes.

However, the development of human consciousness is always a

work in progress. Bit by bit, as our I AM is able to connect more consciously with our lower bodies, it spiritualises them to awaken their spiritual counterparts. This means, for example, that our etheric body is not so bound to the forces of survival, eg, growth and reproduction, freeing it to produce inspired thoughts.

In the case of our astral body, our emotions and actions become refined and we become more imaginative. This is the work of our Spirit Self which has a direct correspondence to our astral body. When our I AM influences our consciousness more than our astral levels do, then our spiritual being takes its rightful place as son or heir in our physical being.

One of the ways we know when our Spirit Self is influencing our being is when we have a greater sense of the fraternity of humanity. Now we develop a consciousness that fosters brotherhood and community. Not the exclusive community of nation, race and creed, or even friends and family, but an embracing love for creation which always includes others. These are the peacemakers.

It is interesting that the sixth and seventh Beatitude speak of God; seeing God and then becoming sons of God. This is because at a certain point in the development of our Consciousness Soul, our Spirit Self becomes involved. It is as if the activity of our Consciousness Soul kick-starts our spiritual regions. One of the reasons for this is that our I AM can also be more active in this region of our being. Our I AM could be compared with the idea of a nucleus of an atom which excites the electrons and influences their activity.

Furthermore, once our I AM has a greater influence in our being, the Christ Impulse within us responds accordingly. This Christ Impulse can then be fostered by our experiences of reverence and awe. When the Christ Impulse becomes active in our Consciousness Soul and Spirit Self we notice that increasingly we are at one with others. We don't want others to agree with us, we don't mind what they think, for we experience how all thoughts are parts of the whole. Our own thoughts become more mobile, quickly able to weave in and around the thoughts of others. In the openness the thoughts of others can shed new light on our own thoughts, assisting us to have a larger vision.

This new ability to see the validity of other people's thoughts creates peace. It is only when we want to hold onto our own thoughts that peace is lost. Usually our ability to allow others to have their own ideas is directly linked to how much we love them. If our love is genuine, filled with the Christ Impulse, then peace prevails.

It is good to be aware, however, that strange things happen as we work on our connection to our I AM. When this connection is only budding, experiencing this new power can give us an inflated idea of our abilities. We feel invincible and unaware that we have a lot more connecting to do. On the other hand, when our connection grows stronger we then begin to experience our inadequacies. Through the Christ Impulse we can balance these opposing tendencies of over-estimating or under-estimating our abilities. It is through the presence of Christ that we can stand as we are, embracing our abilities without overstating or understating them. Without excuses or regrets we are peacemakers – of our own inner forces. As John reports Jesus' words of comfort to us; *I have said this to you, that in me you may have peace. In the world you have tribulation* [distress]; *but be of good cheer, I have overcome the world."* Jn 16:33

Two: No inner peace, no I AM

It is very obvious that our modern world is not peaceful. The so-called peacemakers are those who attempt to impose their will on other people. Everywhere, even in the most spiritual of places, people seek to impose controls on others. Rules and regulations are drawn up to place external parameters on our conduct. These rules are often accepted without consensus because "it is easier to keep the peace" than to question. Questioning also involves the exertion of thorough thinking.

The dictionary even says that peace is about being amiable, agreeable, willing to please, harmonious. It also says that peace is about being tranquil which is much closer to the mark. We can only experience true peace when we are inwardly able to calm ourselves in difficult situations.

John reports how Jesus put it very clearly to his inner circle. *"Peace I leave with you; my peace I give to you; not as the world gives do I give to you. Let not your hearts be troubled, neither let them be afraid."* Jn 14:27

The Greek word for 'leave' is *aphiemi* and it speaks of leaving something of yourself behind. The whole point of Jesus' incarnation on earth was to bring the I AM into the physical and then to leave something of it here. In this way we, as human beings, can then develop our own relationship with our I AM.

Bringing the I AM to earth took quite a bit of doing. Prior to Golgotha we connected with our I AM in a group way, that is what Jehovah is all about. Only a few great initiates were able to have a firsthand experience of their individual I AMs. One of them was Zarathustra and he played a huge part in bringing about this new relationship with our individual I AM. Krishna and Buddha were also very closely involved. It is so interesting to contemplate that when it comes to the I AM there can be no exclusivity of belief – the I AM unites every human, belief speaks of the different paths to it.

These great beings, Zarathustra, Buddha, Krishna all left something of themselves behind which could be used by Jesus when he made himself available to human evolution in the way that he did. All worked together to create an atmosphere on the earth for the peacemakers. So how come we have so little peace? Simply because we have yet to play our part as peacemakers. We have to receive both what was left and what is also being given. This requires that we make ourselves ready so that we are 'in tune' to receive. This can only happen when we use our inner forces to connect with our I AM and express ourselves through it as often as possible in our daily living.

The sole purpose of evolution is for our I AM to enter as fully as possible into our earthly consciousness. Part of this process means that our I AM guides us into testing situations. It is as if it leads us into events which give us the greatest opportunity to exercise our ability to connect with it.

It is not about avoiding contentious situations, it is about dealing with them through our inner peace. When we find ourselves in difficult situations we must exert ourselves to experience this peace; otherwise it is not peace but avoidance and inertia. The world wants us to believe that the outcome, the peacefulness, is the point. The world does not want us to think that the actual inner effort of achieving peace is the prize.

Furthermore, once we learn how to achieve inner peace through inner exertion, we have to keep on doing it, not once or twice but continually in a variety of situations. We have to learn to achieve inner peace easily, often and sooner, whenever our hearts are troubled or afraid.

It is this peacemaking ability that makes us receptive to what Jesus left with us. Not only that, our peacemaking ability adds to the gifts of Jesus. Whatever peacemaking we achieve we leave here like an atmosphere to assist others to connect with their I AM. It is like fuel for the ongoing human endeavour of becoming fully I AM beings.

Each time we allow things to disturb us, each time we are sucked into "creating peace at all cost", we actually destroy peace.

Peace the I AM leaves with us; peace the I AM gives to us. No inner peace, no I AM.

The Beatitudes in the Gospel of St John

Three: Making our I AM real during Lent

> *Now Jesus did many other signs in the presence of the disciples, which are not written in this book; but these are written that you may believe that Jesus is the Christ, the Son of God, and that believing you may have life in his name.*
> Jn 20:30-31

Jesus is the great peacemaker. In the book of Hebrews he is called a Melchizedek priest, Melchizedek meaning the king of peace. His name is I AM. In this name, the I AM, we have life. It is the light of this I AM that must light up the darkness of our being so that we become transparent, vibrant light-beings, full of life.

Each year we make the 40 day journey to Easter. Lent is really a preparation to be called, or given the name of, the Sons of God. Our work in the physical is to perfect our Son of Man consciousness so that, at a certain point of maturity we can awaken our Son of God consciousness. They are like two beings within us and both are a work in progress. Until we start connecting up with our I AM and using it with agility we cannot become the Son of Man. When we do that, we can awaken the Son of God. Peace is key.

Eirenopoios is to make peace, to be friendly and harmonious within ourselves and in our relationships with one another, but also we must strive for harmony with the spiritual worlds. We are so oriented to this physical world that we hardly have a peaceful relationship with the spiritual worlds and the hierarchies guiding our evolution. If we are to be called sons of God we must become more conscious of the consequences of our words and actions for they have a huge impact on the spiritual worlds.

Why is it that we can't speak openly and honestly to people? What is it in us that reacts when someone criticises us? Why can't we simply say, "I know, I could have done better, I could have thought more thoroughly before acting ..." and so on. This is the conflict within us that arises in our fledgling Son of Man consciousness. Perfection glimpsed leads to frustration because we discover that we have to do the hard work to achieve it. We have to be tested again and again so that peacemaking becomes second nature. This is played out in harrowing detail in the journey to the cross.

Lent is a good time to set some goals. We could spend 10 days preparing each of our bodies; physical, etheric, astral and I, for the Son of Man. Working on our physical levels would involve our earthly will. We could decide to take up a physical task for 10 days, like washing up or tidying up regularly, or weeding the garden and so forth. Exercises for our etheric would involve our thinking; perhaps resolving to become more aware of our thoughts instead of letting them flow through our mind aimlessly for the next 10 days. Our astral is about our feeling levels; we could decide to feel more about the news items we see; try to feel the sadness and pain of people. Our I is our spiritual will and we could spend the last 10 days finding ways to become more conscious of our I. For instance, we could resolve to be more objective more often during the day.

By taking on exercises like these we become more conscious of what a large role peace plays in our lives. We will also realise how intricately peace is woven into our will.

We should also ask why 'to believe' *pisteuo* is emphasised? *but these are written that you may believe that Jesus is the Christ, the Son of God, and that believing you may have life in his name.*

John uses this word a lot. For a start, John is urging us to trust that we have an I AM and that it is connecting up with us. If we do some of the work, if we show that we are serious about progressing along the path, then the spiritual worlds will come to our aid. Now this is a leap because most of us can't see these things. Contemporary thinking actually points us away from them.

We have to make the choice to believe or not; we have been given the freewill to do so. Perhaps if we simply said this to ourselves each morning for the 40 mornings of Lent: I will become more conscious of my I AM, my eternal self that has experienced all my incarnations thus far. Can we really believe that this I AM looks down on us and tries to direct us this way and that? What does it feel like to be guided in this way? Perhaps at night when we go to bed we could ask our I AM how co-operative we have been. In this way our I AM becomes more real to us.

Of course, at the same time we should also thank our Guardian

Angel for taking care of things when we are not conscious of our I AM.

Four: Peace through thinking

The peacemakers, those who experience true inner peace, are the ones who can control their thinking and who can assist others to do the same. To be able to control thinking requires an understanding of what thinking really is.

Thinking is a series of mental pictures which we call concepts. When we think, we use concepts developed in the past to understand present things. If we have not developed concepts about something in the past then understanding cannot arise. An Australian Aboriginal woman spoke of seeing a truck for the first time; for her it was a moving rock.

When new concepts come to us we must exert ourselves in order to understand. It is this exertion that creates agility in our thinking and fills it with new concepts. If we continually think the same old thoughts, simply recollecting what we once thought, we are not really thinking at all. These thought patterns cannot embrace the new, trucks remain moving rocks.

Peacemakers can embrace the new, without fear, without tiring and without resistance. For instance, they can see beyond the scientific concept that tells us that thinking happens in our brain. Agile thinking can work with the idea that the brain is simply a physical apparatus that makes thoughts accessible to us. Then we can be open to the notion that thinking is an activity of our soul which is centralised in our etheric body. The etheric body stores our concepts and memories; they become available to us in our soul. So the mental pictures are stored in our etheric body, as if in a book, the pictures become available in our soul as if the book is opened.

The experience of thinking is not limited to our brain either; we must also feel our thoughts with our heart. We fill our thinking with depth and contrast when we involve our heart. Otherwise our thoughts remain abstract, dry and empty. It is our I AM that streams into our dead thoughts to fill them with life. If we cannot engage our I AM in this process our thinking is limited and we are not peaceful.

The eighth Beatitude speaks about how our Spirit Self becomes involved in our consciousness. When our Spirit Self can begin to influence our thinking, real spiritual Imagination arises within us. When this begins to happen we become sons of God. We give life to our dead consciousness that arises from the ideas of the many illusions of our modern world.

This life-giving process is referred to by St John in his prologue. *But to all who received him* (the I AM), *who believed in his name, he* (the I AM) *gave power to become children of God; who were born, not of blood nor of the will of the flesh nor of the will of man, but of God.* Jn 1:12-13

If we combine the natural processes of the earth and involve the spiritual process that our I AM wants us to receive, we become offspring of God. This makes us very important people in the cosmic scheme of things. How would we feel meeting the offspring of the leaders of this world, the U.S. President, the Queen of England? Where does that place the offspring of God!

St Paul speaks of the magnitude of this in his letter to the Romans. *For the creation waits with eager longing for the revealing of the sons of God; for the creation was subjected to futility* (emptiness), *not of its own will but by the will of him who subjected it in hope; because the creation itself will be set free from its bondage to decay and obtain the glorious liberty of the children of God. Rom 8:19-21*

In his lecture on the Sermon on the Mount in 1910 Rudolf Steiner puts it this way. "Therefore, Christ says, "Blessed are those who draw the Spirit Self down into themselves, for they shall become the children of God." This points man upward to higher worlds."

Essentially we must fill the emptiness of our consciousness with active thinking; otherwise the anti-forces will use it as a tool to create mischief. Even though they can have a field day with our empty-headedness, they too wait in eager longer - for they are part of creation - for us to take control. The emptiness is an essential part of our spiritual purpose; we must allow it to be filled with the will from above. The peacemakers then experience the glorious liberty of God's children.

8. BLESSED ARE THOSE WHO ARE PERSECUTED BECAUSE OF RIGHTEOUSNESS, FOR THEIRS IS THE KINGDOM OF HEAVEN. MT 5:10

One: Seeing "I" to "I"

The 'ones having been persecuted', *dediogmenoi* in Greek, indicate the ones who are driven away. Who are we inclined to drive away from us? The ones we have karma with. We have incarnated so many times now that most of the people we come into contact with have a karmic connection to us. This karma needs balancing.

Place this in the context of righteousness, *dikaiosune*, which means justice; being just, balanced and in harmony. In this sense, justice is a continual series of adjustments to restore balance and harmony. It also means that we have the ability to judge when things are 'just right'.

Blessed, Christened, are those who are driven away because they try to balance their karma. They try to make the necessary adjustments with others, but the others drive them away and prevent the adjustments from happening. It's true, isn't it? When the heat is on in our relationships we do everything in our power to drive the situation from us. We try to put as much distance as possible between ourselves and the other person. But this is the grit that creates the pearl.

If we can stand in our I AM and relate to the other person's I AM – see "I" to "I" with them, then in that objectivity it is possible to resolve the karmic situation that our I AM has purposefully placed us in. Now, our I AM doesn't place us in these situations so that we can suffer but so that we have the opportunity to make the choice. Of course, whatever choice we make is the right choice. What is important is that we use our inner determination and actually make a choice. If our choice is to drive the situation away from us then it will return and we will have to face it again.

Some people think that Christ looks after our karma. Not so, he came so that we may have the ability to resolve our own karma. When we are able to stand within the forces of our I AM we will feel our reactions dissolve, even if it is just for a moment, then Christ fills us with peace.

St. John explains the situation quite clearly in chapter 15, specifically in these verses: *This I command you, to love one another. "If the world hates you, know that it has hated me before it hated you. If you were of the world, the world would love its own; but because you are not of the world, but I chose you out of the world, therefore the world hates you. Remember the word that I said to you, 'A servant is not greater than his master.' If they persecuted me, they will persecute you; if they kept my word, they will keep yours also. But all this they will do to you on my account, because they do not know him who sent me. If I had not come and spoken to them, they would not have sin; but now they have no excuse for their sin.* John 15:17-22

When we are "of the world", a natural part of the world, we belong to the group and we are not individuals. We are not connected to our I AM and Christ is but a dormant seed within us. When we connect up with our I AM, and awaken the Christ Impulse within us, we make those who are of the world very uncomfortable and they flee away from us.

Why do they flee? Because through our connection with our I AM we have the courage to face our karma – which also happens to involve them. In these moments "we are chosen" to balance a debt that was created by past actions – ours or theirs. Of course, this can be off-putting to others. Of course, they will want to drive us away from them. If they do this there is no opportunity to resolve our differences. There is no opportunity to experience seeing "I" to "I".

A delicate balance needs to be struck. The one who can connect up with their I AM will always meet the other person on their level. Then, when the two are engaged, the one with greater access to their I AM will look for ways to assist the other person too experience their own I AM. What is striking about this interaction is that the other person is usually expecting different behaviour. They may even be defensive. But when two or more people meet on the level of their I AM, Christ is always there.

"For where two or three are gathered in my name [which is I AM], there I am in the midst of them." Mt 18:20

The righteous ones are those who are brave enough to tackle the balancing that is required if we are to see "I" to "I".

Two: *The importance of remaining neutral*

The blessed are those achieve inner happiness. This inner happiness does not come from the riches and rewards of the physical world. This inner happiness comes from the kingdom of heaven. How do we achieve this kingdom? Not by ascending out of our body, not by negating our body, to have spiritual experiences. Certainly not through ecstasy that can come from meditation or religious experience. We can only experience the kingdom of heaven through our physical body when it is in harmony with our soul and spirit. This is the harmony, the balance, of *dikaiosune* or righteousness.

Harmony of body, soul and spirit means that our thoughts, emotions and behaviour are balanced. Neither one takes prominence. We can think clearly, our reasoning is sound, our feelings are pure and conscious, and our behaviour is noble and contained.

Most of all, we resist the oscillating pattern of like and dislike that is a compelling instinct. It is amazing how many decisions we make each day not based on logic but on what we like or dislike. Our behaviour towards others is so often dictated by our sympathy or antipathy towards them. It would be a good exercise to decide for a whole day to be neutral about each person we meet.

This neutrality allows the other person to be, and then we can accept them for who they are. This gives us the opportunity to experience them more deeply. Very often when people annoy us we never get beyond their annoying behaviour because we are intent on dismissing them from our presence as quickly as possible. We want to remove the annoyance; we want to distance ourselves from annoying behaviour so that we feel better. If we can just live with these feelings that persecute us, if we can find a way to balance the difficult experience, we will have a heavenly reward. We will have become the ruler of our own kingdom and made it a heavenly place.

The kingdom of the heavens, *basileia ton ouranon*, points to a rulership which is raised up. When we control the natural responses that arise in our body and soul we make a space for spirit to speak into us.

The eighth Beatitude is associated with the second region of our spiritual being, the Life Spirit. According to the evolution of the human being we hardly have access to this region of our being. It will not be fully develop for quite some time; however, we must lay the foundation now. Compare it to having driving lessons before we are let loose on the road alone.

The only way we can prepare for this future spiritual expression is to work on the harmony between our body, soul and spirit. The best place to start is to know which parts of our consciousness belong to our body, which parts to our soul and which parts to our spirit. Often we think we are being guided by the spirit and our true inner being when really it is our unconscious feeling levels telling us what feels good. So often we mistake our feelings of like and dislike for our will.

Overwhelmingly, we want to avoid the feelings of persecution that come from our thinking while it tries to balance these unconscious or semiconscious feelings. The fulcrum which can facilitate the balance is our I AM. When we allow the balancing, the righteousness, to work in our being, Christ is aroused.

St. Paul puts it clearly in his letter to the Romans: *But if Christ is in you, although your bodies are dead because of sin, your spirits are alive because of righteousness.* Rom 8:10 St. John reports that Jesus said: *"Truly, truly, I say to you, unless one is born anew* [from above], *he cannot see the kingdom ...."* Jn 3:3

What is above? Our I AM, our human spirit which seeks to be born into our being. When our I AM has access to our etheric body, which means that it has to pass all the way through our astral body to get there, it will raise it up in preparation for it to become our Life Spirit. The first signs of this are when we experience Inspiration which is that spiritual hearing when a kind of silent speech rises up within us to give us spiritual insight. Inspiration also happens when we inspire meaning from our spiritual reading. This means that we have been able to create enough silence within us so that something new can enter. It is through being able to bear the persecution, resisting the need to push things away from us, which gives us access to the kingdom of heaven; we uplift situations through our own rulership.

Three: Kingdom of heaven consciousness

When we express ourselves through our I AM we have a different consciousness. When we allow the Christ Impulse to influence us we have a different consciousness again. Different, that is, from the everyday consciousness of our modern culture. But not different from those who also express themselves from their Christened I AM. This we can call the kingdom of heaven consciousness.

The Gospel of St. John is a manual for navigating modern society with a kingdom of heaven consciousness. Right from the first chapter John points out the difficulties associated with this different consciousness.

The true light - the I AM - was in the world, and the world came into being through the I AM, yet the world did not know the I AM. The I AM entered into individual beings, and the individual beings received it not. Jn 1:9-10

This highlights our natural tendency to prefer the 'same-old', the way things were. Those of us who do manage to express ourselves through our I AM must be prepared to be persecuted by others. When we start to think differently people feel uncomfortable. This is because our feeling levels do not like to be disturbed by thinking. Thinking is exhausting. If someone comes into our environment with a different consciousness, it places demands on us to change our own consciousness, that is, to think differently. How often are we prepared to do that, especially when we are busy, as we often are?

To get the real picture of how difficult it can be to use our I AM consciousness we can look at the events of Jesus' life. He did everything differently. He never checked his calendar when someone needed healing, and very often, it was the wrong day of the week. Like when he told the man to take up his pallet and walk; it turned out to be the sabbath. *The man went away and told the Jews that it was Jesus who had healed him. And this was why the Jews persecuted Jesus, because he did this on the sabbath. Jn 5:15-16*

The Jews can represent our preconceived ideas about how and when things should be done. Something within us enjoys being able to impose controls on others, even if it is just in our own mind. We automatically decide what is right, and what it not right, and then we judge. In their outrage for the individuality of Jesus, the Jews *cried out*, *"Away with him, away with him, crucify him!"* Jn 19:15

The huge question is: how conscious are we of why we make these decisions? Very often, if we examine our ideas in the 'true light', with our I AM consciousness, we realise that it doesn't really matter in the scheme of things. All that really matters is that we move forward towards the wonderful goal of being consciously united with the presence of Christ.

Above all, when others want to persecute us, to drive us away from them (which is what the word 'persecute' means), we must love. If we can do this, the quality of our love fills the universe with the true light. It is our ability to love in this way that makes us co-creators with Christ. Then the kingdom of heaven is ours, wherever we are.

As we accompany Jesus on his journey to the cross, as our consciousness changes with each step, we are able to bear the suffering – gladly even – which transmutes it. Unfortunately, our human nature can place suffering outside us, albeit unconsciously, inflicting hurt on those around us. In this way we crucify others.

It is a most subtle process that we are going through in our consciousness at this point in evolution. While we can at times use the true light of our I AM, at other times we fall back into contemporary consciousness and this creates a tug-of-war tension. We need to develop the ability to be with the tension, to be present with it so that we can think clearly. Through loving eyes, like Jesus, we understand the quantum leap in consciousness that is developing – in us and in those around us. We can also see how, for some, it is very difficult to adjust. Then, in our understanding we can forgive them for wanting to push us away. We can love regardless, as Jesus did, because he was the pioneer of this kingdom of heaven consciousness.

Four: *The persecution within us*

On the surface it seems strange that a person would be persecuted for righteousness. What this Beatitude says is that people flee away from those who are balanced. So this would suggest that the way of the world is for people to be unbalanced. There are forces trying to influence the evolution of the world that prefer human beings to be unbalanced. For when we are balanced, we are able to determine what is right and what isn't. We have an innate sense of justice and morality.

Morality is very misunderstood. It isn't about behaving according to the half-formed ideas of others; it is about love, *agape*, the Christened love that calls from the depth of our being. When it stirs, it is a love that you can't hold back. It flows out in abundance into the hearts of others. St. John gives us a most interesting picture of morality.

The scribes and the Pharisees brought a woman who had been caught in adultery, and placing her in the midst they said to him, "Teacher, this woman has been caught in the act of adultery. Now in the law Moses commanded us to stone such. What do you say about her?" This they said to test him, that they might have some charge to bring against him. Jesus bent down and wrote with his finger on the ground. And as they continued to ask him, he stood up and said to them, "Let him who is without sin among you be the first to throw a stone at her." And once more he bent down and wrote with his finger on the ground. But when they heard it, they went away, one by one, beginning with the eldest, and Jesus was left alone with the woman standing before him. Jesus looked up and said to her, "Woman, where are they? Has no one condemned you?" She said, "No one, Lord." And Jesus said, "Neither do I condemn you; go, and do not sin again." Jn 8:3-11

We can use this story to look at the eighth Beatitude by applying it to our own consciousness. The Scribes and the Pharisees persecute us when they think that we love in the wrong way. The Scribes and the Pharisees can represent the way our modern culture thinks; you can do this but you can't do that. They can also represent our instincts and second hand ideas that we haven't actively thought through ourselves.

So this story is giving us an Imagination of how our being; body

(Scribes and Pharisees), soul (the woman) and spirit (Jesus, the I AM in the process of absorbing the Christ Impulse) is interacting.

When the woman, our soul, wakes up to more of its options there is a kafuffle in our being. Mostly our soul responds to our body in an unconscious way and that is the way the body likes it. When we wake up our soul, our feeling, thinking and behaviour change. They no longer do the bidding of the body's automatic habits, they start to dance to the tune of the I AM. In this case, to express love in ways that the body doesn't think is appropriate.

Our body is much more comfortable sticking to its routine. This means that our soul remains asleep and acts automatically as it has always done. Jesus, the I AM, stirs things up in our soul, arousing it to act independently of the body. The body responds by wanting to stone the soul, threatening it, and wanting to cause damage or even death.

This is where we are at present in evolution. The death of the soul is a very real threat. The evolution of consciousness is in crisis. We could even go further and say that the forces in our bodies, represented in this story by the Scribes and Pharisees, are the anti-forces which we call Ahriman and Lucifer. While we remain unconscious of our I AM, these forces think and feel in us. They take over our idle soul and act out their own ideas in us. They tell us not to experience the fullness of love; they direct our attention away from the Christ Impulse that lies within us like a seed since Golgotha.

All we need to do is to recognise what they are up to. The I AM will bend down and reveal the true nature of things. The I AM is our eternal being; it is the string holding together the pearls of each of our lives. If we can allow the I AM to speak into our being, as John tells us, *"when they heard it, they went away, one by on."* The I AM will never condemn us. Sin is simply being unconscious of our I AM. Once we begin to allow our spirit, our I AM, to work into our soul we must ensure that we continue with that work, then ours is the kingdom of heaven.

9. BLESSED ARE YE, WHEN MEN SHALL REVILE YOU, AND PERSECUTE YOU, AND SAY ALL MANNER OF EVIL AGAINST YOU FALSELY, FOR MY SAKE. REJOICE AND BE EXCEEDING GLAD, FOR GREAT IS YOUR REWARD IN HEAVEN: FOR SO PERSECUTED THEY THE PROPHETS WHICH WERE BEFORE YOU. MT 5:11-12

One: Experiencing the Etheric Images of Golgotha

If we are to truly experience the Christ Impulse within us then we must also experience the Mystery of Golgotha in all its reality.

If we follow the stories in the bible we can see that Jesus evokes reaction wherever he goes and through whatever he does. Some people are deeply affected by him and a renewed need to search arises within them. Others want him removed and killed.

It is a fact that those who do not experience their I AM will always revile (speak abusively), persecute (push away) and say false things (lie) about those who do. Therefore we could say that if we are abused, rejected and lied about it is a sign that we are on the right path.

This doesn't mean to say that if we upset people it indicates that we are progressing. The proof of our progress is when we don't react if we are verbally abused, rejected or lied about. Even if we don't outwardly express our reaction, we must also be able to control our thoughts, feelings and will so that we don't react privately either. Here lies the challenge.

We can meet this challenge if we are able to experience the reality of Golgotha, place ourselves in the sandals of Jesus, for we can use those images to rise above the bad manners of others.

Imagine experiencing the following without flinching! *Then Pilate took Jesus and scourged him. And the soldiers plaited a crown of thorns, and put it on his head, and arrayed him in a purple robe; they came up to him, saying, "Hail, King of the Jews!" and struck him with their hands. Pilate went out again, and said to them, "See, I am bringing him out to you, that you may know that I find no crime in him." So Jesus came out, wearing the crown of thorns and the purple robe. Pilate said to them, "Behold the man!" When the chief priests and the officers saw him, they cried out, "Crucify him, crucify him!" Pilate said to them, "Take him yourselves and crucify him, for I find no crime in him." The Jews answered him, "We have a law, and by that law he ought to die, because he has made himself the Son of God."* Jn 19:1-7

This is what Jesus, the I AM about to be fully united with the Christ Impulse, actually experienced. He was participating in a critical evolutionary process that we must all follow. He was the pioneer, carving out the way. Now we, too, can be like him. Fortunately we don't need to physically go through what he went through; we experience it in our consciousness.

It will be helpful to consider some esoteric facts about human life and death at this point. All the experiences we have during our life are stored in our etheric body as memory. When we die, during the first three days after death, we review these memories. Those etheric forces which we have managed to purify remain in the earth's etheric atmosphere, strengthening it and enhancing the Christ Impulse that is found there since Golgotha.

Because Jesus was able to purify his etheric body to such an extent that the full force of Christ could dwell there, his whole Christ-imbued etheric body remained in the etheric field of this earth. Therefore all the images of Jesus' life are there for us to view as and when we are able. We can access these living images in our contemplations of the accounts in the Gospels. We can set aside our earth-bound thinking, we can intensify our feelings and we can strive to capture a firsthand experience of these living etheric images. This is an awesome gift which we can receive if we are able.

However, we must be aware that there are opposing forces that do not want us to have this Easter experience. The closer we come to the images, the stronger the distractions.

It doesn't matter what difficult experiences we have to go through to be united with our I AM and to experience the living presence of the Christ Impulse within us and within the etheric sphere of this earth. If the images of Golgotha become alive in our consciousness and readily accessible, we will not be distracted from our goal. We will rejoice and be glad at every opportunity to connect up with Golgotha and its mighty purpose.

Two: Creating community

There is no greater task for us than to create community with others. This is a most crucial time in evolution and this Beatitude points directly to it. How can we create community and fraternity in an atmosphere of verbal abuse, persecution and lies? Sadly, we don't have to look far to find people behaving in this way towards others, even if only in their thoughts.

This ninth Beatitude is about developing our highest spiritual expression, Spirit Man. This happens when our I AM can penetrate our physical body and raise it, resurrect it. Then we will have fulfilled human destiny. We will have become fully human and fully divine. Although we are far from this point, we are preparing the groundwork, especially since we are currently developing our highest soul region, the Consciousness Soul. There is a connection here because both the Consciousness Soul and Spirit Man are connected with our physical body and our will. Our will of course governs our behaviour. It is through exercising our will that we curb any inclination to think or act badly towards others.

If we look at a child who is discovering his or her will we can make a direct link to this stage in the evolution of human consciousness. The child must go through a period of controlling their will before they can use it responsibly. So too, as human beings we must govern our will so that our behaviour is community-creating. We could say that the present challenges of creating community with others directly points to the evolutionary development of our will. Can we resist the unconscious memories of antipathy that rise up within us when we interact with some people?

If we look around in the world today we quickly see that this phase of evolution carries with it a feeling of desolation for many people. They feel alone and lonely without a sense of community. This results from the underlying experience of persecution, of wanting to flee away from all that distresses us. As well, anxiety and depression are experienced by increasing numbers of people.

While we can agree that this is a dismal outlook, at the same time it does point to hope for the future. The feeling of separation arises within us when we become aware of the life of our soul. When we turn away from purely materialistic concepts and experience the life of our soul we must then push onwards and become aware of our spirit. This can be accompanied by a feeling of being lost. We face things that are foreign, that our culture has not made familiar for us. We can be left searching as many people today are searching.

What is the nature of this searching? Usually we search for instant gratification, for readymade solutions. Yet the secret of the quest is that it is up to us to find the solution, to strive for it. It cannot come to us from outside, not from other people nor government policy nor any kind of philosophy. Even Christ who dwells within us and permeates everything since Golgotha cannot give us the answer. The only way to find the solution is through our own thinking. The kind of energetic and original thinking that comes from connecting with our I AM. Christ doesn't do this for us; he simply gives us the possibility to do it.

The best way to generate this kind of thinking is by connecting up with others, by building community. This means that we must resist any antipathy that creeps up through our feelings because that arrests our thinking. We must use our will to be open to the ideas of others, to listen to them, to allow their ideas to enter into us. Whether we agree or not is beside the point. Even if we don't understand them or even if what they say is difficult to bear, when we listen to others, when we allow them to enter into us, a bond is created, a feeling of community arises. This all happesns in an atmosphere of free will.

Community-creating occurs by overcoming ourselves. Through the efforts of each single person we build communities through what we have in common. When we can do this we experience the Christ Impulse in ourselves while at the same time contributing to the Christ Impulse in the world. We can say to others (or at least think it), even to those who abuse us, push us away or lie about us, "Christ is in you as he is in me, if we can experience the reality of this we can create true community with each other." There can be no greater reward than to experience the Christ Impulse alive within us and within those around us. We fulfil those powerful words, *"This is my commandment, that you love one another as I have loved you."* Jn 15:12

Three: Handling everything with gratitude

It is difficult to get a picture of how we could rejoice and be glad when others abuse and repel us and even lie about us. It would not be a wise response to start smiling, laughing and dancing around the person who is treating us badly. They would see this as taunting and could possibly become enraged. This is actually a reality today, especially on the roads. If someone abuses us and we laugh at them this can escalate into road rage.

No, this rejoicing, *chairo*, is an inner experience. The gladness, *agalliao*, means to be exalted, spiritually elevated, beyond our instinctive natural behaviour.

Quietly, within us, we respond differently and gratitude arises. Not gratitude that the other person was rude to us, but gratitude that we can handle it. When we have a genuine experience of being able to deal with verbal abuse etc. we have every reason to rejoice. This genuine response, not simply masking our reaction, is spiritual exaltation which has become an integral part of us.

Because this Beatitude is about the will, this new habit means that there is no longer any physical change in our body when we receive abuse; we don't turn red with anger for instance. We respond with what the bible calls "God's will" which is really our true will. This higher, refined will is available to us when we connect with our I AM.

John gives us an idea of how this might work when he reports the departing Jesus' words to his disciples:

When a woman is in travail she has sorrow, because her hour has come; but when she is delivered of the child, she no longer remembers the anguish, for joy that a child is born into the world. So you have sorrow now, but I will see you again and your hearts will rejoice, and no one will take your joy from you. Jn 16:21-22

When we start aligning ourselves with the Christ Impulse, as the disciples did, our soul becomes pregnant with Christ. As we nurture and nourish the infant forces within us they displace our automatic physical responses to the outside world. This is the story of the spiritual responses associated with our will. In this process three things are happening; we are gestating the Christ Impulse, we are preparing to receive the influence of our I AM and we are awakening our soul from its dull, daily drudge. This obviously unsettles us and we also become an unsettling influence in the world.

Our responses become more unpredictable, and people prefer predictability. (Although in reality they don't, for predictability breeds boredom.) It is as if the will is tugging at us; on one side urging us towards the predictable but on the other side towards excitement and daring. We become aware of an unconscious will-response within us to the presence of Christ; will we retreat or charge. These experiences are directly related to our connection with our I AM and the freedom of will that accompanies it. Our challenge is to take the middle road. It is the Christ Impulse that assists us to achieve the inner balance.

John continues ... *In that day you will ask nothing of me. Truly, truly, I say to you, if you ask anything of the Father, he will give it to you in my name. Hitherto you have asked nothing in my name; ask, and you will receive, that your joy may be full.* Jn 16:23-24

And we don't do that, do we? Just as Jesus said, we ask nothing of him. Jesus, the prototype, the pioneer, is available to be asked! Ask and you will receive he says!

Whenever we must deal with difficult situations, especially when people do not understand our unsettling ways, we could sit quietly and ask Jesus for guidance. We could ask him to share with us how he lived his life, especially during the years between the baptism and the cross.

What does Jesus really mean when he says, "ask in my name"? Does he mean the name 'Jesus' or the name 'I AM' – which is our name too? He is saying that if we use this name I AM we will receive.

When we express ourselves through our I AM we are automatically aligned with the Christ Impulse and people will abuse us as they abused Jesus - "on my account" he says. By this stage, however, we have tasted the sweet success that comes from our true will. This is the great reward in heaven.

Four: *Know thyself*

The nine Beatitudes give us clues to the changes that occur in our consciousness as we connect with our I AM and awaken the Christ Impulse within us. This is not a prescribed process, we are individuals. We have looked at how each Beatitude speaks about the nine members of our being. These members are interwoven, each one mobile to a varying extent. According to our striving, these members become more and more mobile and consciously available to us.

We call this self-knowledge. Through self-knowledge we come to recognise how the Christ Impulse transforms us. This is our purpose in life. Christ depends on us to become aware of his Impulse within us and thereby become co-creators with him. If he didn't need us, he would have already done the job.

The Beatitudes show very clearly that we can only develop our consciousness in the presence of opposition. It is the overcoming of the obstacles that produces the results. Each time we succeed our consciousness is transformed. These obstacles usually present themselves as karma. It follows that the more we work through the higher levels of our being the more challenging will be the karma.

If we react when we are reviled, rejected or lied about, we play into the hands of karma so to speak. We must come to realise that within us our memory impels us to respond in a particular way. We carry within us so many unconscious memories from this life and past lives. These memories inform our behaviour and we can often act automatically in situations. We know this is true because we can often predict how others will behave when placed in a certain situation.

Our karma is like a current beneath the surface of our daily life. Its purpose is not to bug us but to assist us to become consciously aware self-realised individuals. As long as we react predictably to the way some people treat us we do not have self-knowledge. It is not until we become conscious of our karmic challenges that we can act out of our freewill. Karma will pull us in one direction, time and time again until we can delay our response long enough to become conscious of what is at work. Then our thoughts raise the way we feel to a higher level and we modify our behaviour.

In this last Beatitude Jesus is comparing us to the prophets. These are the ones who have a firsthand experience of spiritual truth. Jesus is also saying that the time has passed for prophets, we no longer need them, they were "before us". Now we can all have a firsthand experience of our I AM and through the Christ Impulse we can know all things. John puts this most clearly:

"Now we know that you [the I AM] *know all things, and need none to question you; by this we believe that you came from God."* Jn 16:30

We are part of a new vision. Each individual human being is capable of expressing him or herself through their I AM. As this new vision gradually reveals itself and the new consciousness belongs to only a few, those still using the old consciousness will be very unsettled and will say unpleasant things. To assist us through this process John gives us three reassuring Beatitudes of his own. Whenever we are unsettled we can reflect on them.

So they took branches of palm trees and went out to meet him, crying, *"Hosanna!* **Blessed is he who comes in the name of the Lord [I AM]**, *even the King of Israel!"* Jn 12:13 16

Truly, truly, I say to you, a servant is not greater than his master; nor is he who is sent greater than he who sent him. If you know these things, **blessed are you if you do them** [**act out of our I AM**]. Jn 13:16-17

Jesus said to him, "Have you believed because you have seen me? **Blessed are those who have not seen and yet believe."** Jn 20:29

It is up to us come in the name, the I AM, and to know that we stand with Christ as his co-worker. We do not need physical proof of his external presence; we now experience his presence within us.

This brings our contemplations of the Beatitudes to a close. Some say there are ten and align them with the Ten Commandments, others say there are eight, aligning them with Buddha's Eightfold Path; nine therefore is the balance. If the Beatitudes speak of anything, they speak of balance, of the third way.

OTHER WORKS BY THE AUTHOR

Print publication

I Connecting : The Soul's Quest ISBN 978-0-9779825-3-0
www.i-connecting.com published by Goldenstone Press July 2007
Published as an ebook in Kindle 2012 under the title
I AM The Mystery
Workbook and workshop associated with this work
http://i-connecting.com/Workbook
http://i-connecting.com/Workshop

Reflection series by Kristina Kaine

Kindle and Paperback

1. I AM The Soul's Heartbeat. Volume 1
The Seven I AM Sayings in St John's Gospel: 2003

2. I AM The Soul's Heartbeat. Volume 2
Christian Initiation in St John's Gospel: 2003 – 2004

3. I AM The Soul's Heartbeat. Volume 3
Finding the Eightfold Path of Buddha in St John's Gospel: 2004

4. I AM The Soul's Heartbeat. Volume 4
The Twelve Disciples in St John's Gospel: 2005

5. I AM The Soul's Heartbeat. Volume 5
The Seven Signs in St John's Gospel: 2006

6. I AM The Soul's Heartbeat. Volume 6
The Beatitudes in St John's Gospel: 2006 – 2007

7. The Soul's Secret Unveiled in the Book of Revelation: 2007 – 2010
2 volumes ebook, 1 volume print

8. I AM The Soul's Heartbeat. Volume 7
The Bible Unlocked: 2009 –

9. Who is Jesus : What is Christ : 2010 –

10. I AM Exercises 2013

Kristina writes regularly about her understanding of the human soul and spirit. She is an associate director of Spiritual Science Bible Studies which distributes her weekly Reflections.

You can read more about her at the following websites.
http://www.spiritualsciencebiblestudies.org/
http://www.facebook.com/EsotericConnection
http://www.soulquesting.wordpress.com/
http://www.bibleunlocked.blogspot.com.au/
http://www.esotericconnection.com/
http://www.i-connecting.com/

ABOUT THE AUTHOR

Kristina Kaine has worked with people all her life: during her early career in medical sales and staff recruitment, and for the last 20 years in her own business which matches people in business partnerships, as well as for home sharing and home minding. Through this rich interaction with people, Kristina has observed the struggle for self identity from many angles. She was awakened to the ideas of Rudolf Steiner by Rev Mario Schoenmaker, attending all of Schoenmaker's lectures for 14 years.

After Schoenmaker's death in 1997, Kristina realised the need to explain the knowledge of the threefold human being in simple terms that could be applied easily in daily life. As well as her weekly reflections that are read worldwide, she has set this out in her book, 'I Connecting : the Soul's Quest', which was published in 2007 by Robert Sardello. It is not unusual for her to receive comments about her book like this: "It seems like a very lucid treatment, like looking through a clear glass window through which one can discover and recognize the landscape of the soul."

Made in the USA
Columbia, SC
16 May 2022